MAP NO. 1

The journey from Kazusa to the Capital

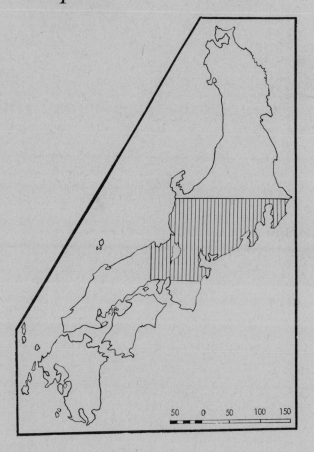

AS I CROSSED
A BRIDGE OF DREAMS

Recollections of a Woman in Eleventh-Century Japan

London | Oxford University Press | 1971

AS I CROSSED
A BRIDGE OF DREAMS

Recollections of a Woman in Eleventh-Century Japan

Translated from the Japanese by *Ivan Morris*

To Sir Hugh and Lady Casson

Oxford University Press, Ely House, London W. 1

GLASGOW   NEW YORK   TORONTO   MELBOURNE   WELLINGTON
CAPE TOWN   SALISBURY   IBADAN   NAIROBI   DAR ES SALAAM
LUSAKA   ADDIS ABABA   BOMBAY   CALCUTTA   MADRAS   KARACHI
LAHORE   DACCA   KUALA LUMPUR   SINGAPORE   HONG KONG   TOKYO

Published in the United States of America by The Dial Press, New York
• Published in the United Kingdom by Oxford University Press, London • ISBN 0-19-212553-2

Contents

Illustrations,
Photographs,
and
Maps

Maps

(See Introduction, p. 11)

Sections and Chronology

· b. 1008

1021 = Lady S = 13

marriage in 1044?

One thousand years ago a woman in Japan with no name wrote a book without a title. All that we know is contained in this brief volume, which by chance survived the centuries of civil war and conflagration. Though neglected for many centuries, it is now firmly entrenched as one of the early Japanese classics. Parts of it are required reading for Japanese school children, and the book is known (though not necessarily read) by every educated person in the country.

The author belonged to the extraordinary group of literary women that flourished in Japan during the tenth and eleventh centuries. These women had a great deal of leisure, they were educated, and their social position was favourable; above all, they had the advantage of using a pure Japanese language rather than the Sino-Japanese hybrid favoured by male literati of the time. From their indefatigable brushes flowed works like *The Tale of Genji* and *The Pillow Book*, which now, a millennium later, still rank among Japan's proudest achievements, while the laborious writings of their male contemporaries are read by few people except scholars. As has been well pointed out, "such overwhelming literary predominance of women is a rare, if not unique, phenomenon in [the world's] cultural history."

With the notable exception of *The Tale of Genji* the writing of these women is intensely personal. In their notes and letters and recollections they reveal themselves to us in all their nakedness, describing each nuance of feeling, each intimate hope, each secret disappointment. Yet there are also great lacunae: for all the emotional and aesthetic detail we frequently cannot tell whether they were married, what children they had, where they lived, who supported them in their leisure, or when and how they had their meals. Sometimes we do not even know what they were called.

So it is with the author of this book. She is usually known as "Takasue's Daughter" (Takasue no Musume), much as if

Madame de Lafayette and George Eliot were to have no other names but the Daughter of de la Vergne or Evan's Daughter. Sugawara no Takasue was a humdrum provincial official, whose name would soon have been buried in the slagheap of history had it not been for his gifted daughter and the chance circumstances that preserved her book. I prefer to call her Lady Sarashina; for, though she would never have recognized this name herself, Sarashina is the title that was given to her little book, and it is by her book that we know her.

Lady Sarashina, like most other famous women writers of the time, belonged to the so-called Heian middle class. By this we should not imagine some burgeoning group of thrifty, hard-working merchants, sturdily asserting themselves against the dominant aristocracy, but a category of officials and their families, themselves often of aristocratic descent, who occupied ranks below the ruling stratum of High Court Nobles and above the mass of petty functionaries and commoners.

It was from this class that men were normally recruited to go and govern the distant provinces. Such assignments, though often lucrative, were usually unwelcome, being regarded as a banishment; for they involved prolonged absence from the capital city of Heian Kyō (Kyoto), the centre of all good things. No one tarred with the brush of the provinces was likely to advance above the Fifth Rank in the Court hierarchy. Lady Sarashina's father ended his career as Assistant Governor of Hitachi (Senior Fifth Rank, Lower Grade), her husband was finally appointed Governor of Shinano (Junior Fifth Rank, Upper Grade), and her son became Provisional Governor of Chikugo (Junior Fifth Rank, Lower Grade).

Though scorned by the high aristocracy, the members of the middle class made vital contributions to Heian culture. Takasue himself came from a long line of distinguished literary men. His ancestor in the ninth century was Michizane, the famous scholar-statesman, whose political defeat by the ruling Fujiwara family ensured that he would forever be counted among Japan's heroes but barred his descendants from power. More recent ancestors had distinguished academic titles, including Rector of the University and Doctor of Literature.

On her mother's side Lady Sarashina belonged to a minor branch of the prepotent Fujiwaras, descending from the great chieftain who, some two centuries earlier, had established the supremacy of the Northern House. In Sarashina's time this House continued to dominate the government in the name of a succession of young and politically impotent emperors; but her connexion with the top-ranking Fujiwaras was far too tenuous to have any practical value for herself or for her relations. The family of Lady Sarashina's mother included a number of well-known writers. By far the most illustrious was her sister, who had been the secondary wife of Kaneie, one of the Fujiwara bigwigs; the sister's infatuation for this man and the misery caused her by his neglect and infidelity are the subject of *Kagerō Nikki*, in which she pours out all her bitterness and frustration, resulting in one of the most intense studies of jealousy ever written.* Arthur Waley stresses the influence of this work on subsequent Heian literature, notably on *The Tale of Genji*; and Lady Sarashina must certainly have read it. Typically enough, however, we have no idea of the author's name. Her designation, as casual as that of her famous niece, is simply "Michitsuna's Mother." It would almost seem that the extraordinary achievements of Heian women writers provoked an unconscious resentment among male scholars, with the result that these talented ladies were permanently condemned to anonymity.

Our budget of knowledge about Lady Sarashina's outer life

*There is a full translation by Professor E. G. Seidensticker, *The Gossamer Years* (Tokyo: Tuttle Co., 1964).

is slim. She was born in 1008 at the very height of the Heian Period, shortly after Sei Shōnagon's *Pillow Book* was completed and while Lady Murasaki was still working on her monumental novel. Lady Sarashina's early years were spent in the refulgent capital of Heian Kyō (the present Kyoto), but we know nothing about them. Then at the age of nine she was taken with her family to a province in the eastern wilds of Japan where her father had been posted as Assistant Governor. When she was twelve years old they all returned to the Capital, and her book starts with a description of the three-month journey to the West. We thus have a vivid picture of how the Japanese countryside appeared to an observant young girl at the time of King Canute. It is a rather breathless account and we could wish for more continuous detail; but none of the other Heian ladies left records of their travels in the provinces, and there is nothing like it in other literatures of the world at this period of history.

Lady Sarashina then settled in the Capital with her family and, apart from frequent pilgrimages to outlying temples, she remained there for the rest of her life. We are told nothing about her education, but from her book we know that she must have studied poetry and also that she was an avid reader of Japanese fiction.

In 1021, when Lady Sarashina was thirteen, her nurse died in an epidemic. This was a cruel blow; but a far greater shock came two years later when her elder sister died in childbirth. Partings, deaths, and expectations of death punctuate the book and took a heavy emotional toll. Like Murasaki Shikibu and the characters in *The Tale of Genji*, Lady Sarashina seems to have had a remarkably low tolerance for bereavement and found it hard to recuperate:

Ever since I was a child the news of people's death, even the death of strangers, had disturbed me greatly and it used to take a long time to recover from the shock. How shattering then was the death of my own sister!

A few years earlier she had been plunged into grief over the death of a young Fujiwara lady whom she had never even met but whose calligraphy she admired ("The sight of these verses, which she had copied in her remarkably beautiful hand, brought on a fresh fit of weeping"). An awareness of life's evanescence and of the poignant nature of the human condition was the mark of any emotionally cultivated member of the Heian upper class. Lady Sarashina's unhappiness, however, was not the stylish melancholy affected by many of her courtly contemporaries but sprang from some deep well in her own timid, hypersensitive nature. Perhaps a clue is provided in the early part of the book by the repeated references to loss and departure: "At the thought of abandoning [the statue] I began weeping quietly to myself"; "After she left I yearned for her and wept silently day after day"; "How sad it would be to leave this place even though we had been here for only a few days!"; "I, being young and impressionable, was particularly moved by the scene and, when the time came, did not want to leave the shelter of our hut." As time after time one finds Lady Sarashina wilted with grief one cannot help wishing her a modicum of Sei Shōnagon's tough insouciance and humour: it would have made her journey far easier.

After the death of Lady Sarashina's sister her closest relationship was with her father. Indeed, apart from the author herself, Takasue is the only character who stands out clearly in the book, and some readers may even be tempted to detect a sort of father fixation. Takasue emerges as a querulous, self-centered old whiner; but it is clear that his daughter loved him dearly. At the age of about sixty he finally received another appointment, again to one of the unpopular eastern provinces. This time he left his family in the capital, and his departure plunged Lady Sarashina into a new slough of misery. Neither of them expected to meet again; in fact he returned safely at the end of his four-years' term. His daughter, who at twenty-eight had long passed the normal Japanese age for marriage, continued living at home, a shy, secluded spinster, whose main duty was to look after her orphaned nieces.

At the age of thirty-one she finally took the plunge and left to become a lady-in-waiting to one of the Imperial Princesses. From the outset it was obvious that she had started far too late to make a success at Court, and she was never called to serve in the Imperial Palace itself. Her dreamy, retiring nature made it hard to hold her own with the other ladies (one can imagine how she would have fared at the hands of a Sei Shōnagon); and besides she was constantly obliged to return home because of her father's complaints of loneliness. Nonetheless she continued as a lady-in-waiting at the Princess's Court on and off for about five years. When she was thirty-four she developed a romantic infatuation for an elegant young courtier whom she met on a dark, rainy night, and who appears to have won her heart less by his appearance (for she really never saw him) than by his lyrical description of the seasons. Marriage would have been out of the question because he was far too grand (he attained the empyrean heights of Junior Second Rank); but a more sexually enterprising woman like Lady Izumi or Lady Nijō would probably have taken him as a lover. As it was, the relationship remained insubstantial and it petered out within a year.

She was eventually married at about thirty-six, which for a woman in Heian times was almost old age. Her husband, six years her senior, was a typical member of the "middle class" and had already served as Governor of Shimotsuke Province. He appears to have been a tolerant, good-natured man, but we can tell little from the book since Lady Sarashina hardly mentions him. A son was born about a year after the marriage, and later she had two more children; but they too are passed over without a single description.

During the years following her marriage Lady Sarashina's main interest in life appears to have been pilgrimages. In Heian times they were the usual pretext for travelling; and it is clear that for Lady Sarashina, as for most of her Courtly contemporaries, the long journeys to the temples were not primarily religious—unless of course we accept the worship of nature as a form of religion. An expedition to Hase, which one can now reach by car from Kyoto in a couple of hours, required several arduous days of travel in Lady Sarashina's time and, as we know from her diary, these trips were not only uncomfortable but dangerous. Yet she went back again and again to Hase, Kurama, Ishiyama, and the other country temples, partly to escape the uncongenial realities of life in the Capital, partly in belated compliance with the warnings she had received in her dreams, but most of all, I think, for the joy she derived from the ever-changing beauties of the Yamato countryside, a joy that endured long after she had abandoned her illusions about mundane success, family life, and the roseate world of romances.

Fortunately for us, this restless pilgrim kept a record of her expeditions, and her book is one of the first extant examples of the typically Japanese *genre* of travel writing, in which descriptions of the countryside are interspersed with anecdotes, reflexions, and lyrical poems, the entire journey of course being regarded as a metaphor to describe life itself.

For all her interest in travel, Lady Sarashina was remarkably ignorant about Japanese geography. She makes several mistakes about the places she visits and, when her husband was appointed to an important central province, she seems to have had only the vaguest idea where it was. This is part of a general indifference to objective conditions in the outside world. Her interest in this world was limited to what impinged directly on her own emotional and aesthetic concerns. She lived in troubled times when the country was faced with the first unmistakable signs that the system of central government, which had lasted for some four centuries, was being violently challenged. And the challenges came not from some remote land beyond the seas, but from the provinces with which Lady Sarashina's class was most closely associated. In 1028 a large-scale insurrection broke out in the province of Kazusa, where she had spent her childhood, and it took the government three years to bring it under control. Lady Sarashina appears to have been quite oblivious of this revolt, if indeed she ever heard about it, and continued busily writing about the mist-shrouded moon and the rustling of bamboo leaves. In 1051, the year in which she describes her delightful trip to Izumi, fierce fighting broke out in the northern provinces. Again the government had to depend on an outside military family to subdue the rebels, since the imperial forces were ineffective; this led to the so-called Early Nine Years' War, which in fact lasted twelve years, bringing about revolutionary changes in the provincial power structure. These rumblings presaged the collapse of the centralized political and social structure on which Heian culture was based; yet there is not the faintest reverberation in Lady Sarashina's book. Nor do any of the other Court ladies, however gifted and observant, evince the slightest interest in the world that lay beyond their direct emotional and aesthetic ken. Shōnagon, Murasaki, Izumi and the others represent almost the entire gamut of feminine character and temperament; yet they are alike in concentrating on a limited range of human experience. This helps explain the curiously patchy impression we get from reading their works: it is like seeing a garden at night in which certain parts are lit up so brightly that we can distinguish each blade of grass, each minute insect, each nuance of colour, while the rest of the garden and the tidal wave that threatens it remain in darkness.

When Lady Sarashina was forty-nine, her husband received a new appointment, and after the usual elaborate preparations set out for the East. Their eldest son, now aged about twelve, accompanied him; but Lady Sarashina, for reasons that we can readily surmise, remained in the Capital. In contrast to her wild grief when her father had left for the provinces, her feelings about her husband's departure seem cool, even detached. This time, though confronted with a most sinister omen, she had no foreboding of death; yet this time death came. After only half a year in his province her husband returned, presumably because of illness, and some months later she "lost him like a dream."

Despite her apparent indifference to him when he was alive, his death was an appalling loss and she never seems to have recovered. Perhaps, like so many women, she preferred the idea of a husband to the concrete husband himself. Her children offered little consolation, and she rarely saw any members of her family. Probably it was during this last, lonely period that she wrote her book. The record fades out sadly a few years later when Lady Sarashina was in her fifties. We know nothing about her end, but I am inclined to imagine that her final months were spent alone in the safety of some peaceful hillside temple near Heian Kyō.

Though the formal biographical note that follows Lady Sarashina's book credits her with other works, including the famous *Hamamatsu Chūnagon Monogatari* ("Tale of Counsellor Hamamatsu"), the evidence of her authorship is dubious, and we should base our picture of the woman entirely on *Sarashina Nikki* and her poems. In almost every respect she was the antithesis of her near-contemporary, Sei Shōnagon, the witty, ebullient author of *The Pillow Book*. They would surely have loathed each other had they met. Lady Sarashina was naïve, timorous, introspective, solitary. Though kind and affectionate by nature, she had difficulty in asserting her emotions, and until the end one senses something ineffectual and irresolute about her, not only in personal relations but in her entire approach to the outside world. She had a few women friends, with whom she carried on sporadic exchanges of poems; but she seems to have been shy with men and intimidated by all strangers, especially at Court. It is true that even Shōnagon was frightened by her first experience of Court life, but she adapted herself to its challenges and was soon lording it over her fellow ladies-in-waiting. Lady Sarashina, who started service when she was a good deal older than Shōnagon, never got over her initial timidity and was clearly a failure in society. Marriage also seems to have come too late in her life, psychologically and perhaps physically too. Despite all her resolutions the comforts of religion appear to have eluded her just as much as the joys of social and family life. Her vague dissatisfactions and yearnings persisted even after her children were born; and her repeated journeys to the countryside were a search for the solace she could find neither at home nor in the Palace.

Thwarted and saddened by the real world, with all its deaths and partings and frustrations, Lady Sarashina protected herself by a barrier of fantasy. Her girlish craving for romantic tales, which for a time became almost obsessive ("I plunged into the Tales and read them day and night. Then I was eager for more . . ."), was an attempt to escape from harsh reality into a rosier, more congenial realm. Many young Heian girls no doubt shared a fascination for romances (Tamakazura in *The Tale of Genji* "spent all day reading and copying romances"); but Lady Sarashina's passion for these books continued long after she had grown up. *The Tale of Genji* was her great joy, and she was forever imagining herself in the role of the tragic young heroine, Lady Ukifune:

The height of my aspirations was that a man of noble birth, perfect in both looks and manners, someone like Shining Genji in the Tale, would visit me just once a year in the mountain village where he would have hidden me like Lady Ukifune. There I should live my lonely existence, gazing at the blossoms and the Autumn leaves and the moon and the snow, and wait for an occasional splendid letter from my lover. This was all I wanted . . .

Of course nothing of the sort could possibly come the way of someone so unsure and retiring. Yūgao and Ukifune might well be her romantic ideals; but Lady Sarashina had none of the recklessness that was needed for a passionate love affair. And (who knows?), perhaps she was not attractive enough either. So it was all sublimated into shadowy longings about handsome princes and moonlit encounters, while reality itself became more and more unreal. In a sense *The Tale of Genji* and the other tales that she so hungrily devoured as a young girl played the same role in her life as did the literary fantasies about Mary Stuart and Agnès Sorel for Flaubert's romance-ridden heroine.

Elle aurait voulu vivre dans quelque vieux manoir, commes ces châtelaines au long corsage qui, sous le trèfle des ogives, passaient leurs jours, le coude sur la pierre et le menton dans la main à regarder venir du fond de la campagne un cavalier à plume blanche qui galope sur un cheval noir.

For both women the gap between dream and reality became a chasm; but Lady Sarashina, as she pictures herself in her book, was far too ethereal, unsexual, and timid to abandon herself in the equivalent of the red plush hotel bedroom in Rouen; and her sufferings always remained relegated to a spiritual plane.

A final escape was in the world of dreams. Dreams are important in Buddhist imagery as a metaphor for the illusory nature of human experience: "All the manifold changes of Karma are but the passing phases of a dream." They also loom large in much Japanese secular literature from *The Tale of Genji* until the works of recent novelists like Kawabata Yasunari. Lady Sarashina's book is the earliest in which dreams are central. As Ikeda Kikan, one of the greatest classical scholars of our time, has written, "The author of *Sarashini Nikki* can be regarded as the first person in Japa-

nese literature to have discovered dreams . . . Her dreams are no
fortuitous interludes but are consciously grasped as having a defi-
nite, inevitable meaning." In its short compass the book describes
about a dozen separate dreams. As we know from our latter-day
experts, dreams normally accompany all sleep and have an essential therapeutic value, so that a "deep, dreamless sleep" is not only
an improbable occurrence but a rather unhealthy one. The great
difference between people in this respect is not whether they
dream but the particular types of dream they recall or claim to
have recalled. The ones that Lady Sarashina records occurred almost entirely in temples, were mainly concerned with unfulfilled
religious duties, and often involved encounters with members of
the opposite sex, from the handsome priest in the first dream, who
ordered her to learn the Lotus Sutra, to the six-foot Amida with
the golden light and the outstretched hands who appeared near
the end of the book and promised to return and fetch her. Lady
Sarashina evidently attached great importance to these dreams
and remembered some of them in detail years after they took
place; indeed it seems likely that she recorded them on waking
up, much as recommended by J. W. Dunne in *Experiment with
Time*. Though usually elated on awaking, she never told anyone
about her dreams and she blithely disregarded their instructions.
Towards the end of her life, however, she recognized the prophetic nature of the earlier dreams and blamed much of her unhappiness on having failed to do as she was told. One hesitates to
indulge in amateur analysis, especially regarding a Court lady
who lived in Japan a thousand years ago; but the dreams that Lady
Sarashina recorded in her book suggest a strong connexion between guilt, religion, sex, and the world of fantasy; and this in
turn may help explain some of the patterns in her waking life.

The book is usually known as *Sarashina Nikki*, though some
scholars insist that it should be *Sarashina no Niki*. Whatever the

proper reading may be, Lady Sarashina herself never gave the book any such title. Like most literary works of the period, it was named by subsequent copyists and scholars for purposes of identification. Sarashina is a mountainous district in central Japan. It is not mentioned a single time in the book; but there is an indirect allusion to the place in one of the author's last poems, and for some reason it was chosen for the title.

Nikki (literally "day-record") is usually translated "diary" or "journal"; but this is an inappropriate description not only for the present book but for most of the other famous *nikki* like *Izumi Shikibu Nikki* and *Kagerō Nikki*. The sense of *genre* has always been fluid in Japanese literature. Particularly in the Heian period the lines of demarcation between novels, romance, story collection, autobiography, journal, memoir, notebook, and poetry collection were most tenuous, and often the same book was variously designated, as for example Lady Izumi's book, which is called both *Izumi Shikibu Nikki* and *Izumi Shikibu Monogatari*.

Even the most cursory reading of *Sarashina Nikki* will show that it is no daily record of events but a book in which the material has been deliberately selected and shaped to reveal certain significant aspects of a woman's life. Dates are rarely provided; though we have a good idea of when most of the events took place, this is the result of painstaking investigation by later scholars, which would have been unnecessary in the case of a proper diary. As the author herself points out, there are often large gaps between the events described. Unlike other Heian *nikki*, the book covers the entire span of Lady Sarashina's lifetime from girlhood to old age; but she has deliberately illuminated certain facets of this life, such as travels and deaths and dreams, while leaving in complete darkness such central events as her marriage and the birth of her children, which could hardly be omitted from a journal. It is precisely this selectivity that makes the book a work of literature rather than a mere record of facts or a collection of random jottings. In her youth, works of romantic fiction had often been more important for Lady Sarashina than the "real" world about her; now in *Sarashina Nikki* she deliberately shaped the events of her actual life into a sort of Tale. The modern Japanese genre it most resembles is the ever-popular *shi-shōsetsu* or "I-novel," in which the author uses the facts of his own life to create a work of quasifiction. The confessional, autobiographical strain has always been particularly strong in Japanese writing, and a book like Lady Sarashina's, which has no real Western equivalent, is in the mainstream of Japan's literary tradition.

When it comes to finding an English title, *The Sarashina Diary* is of course a misnomer, giving an entirely false impression of the book; *Lady Sarashina's Notebook*, though closer to the mark, makes the work appear far too casual and desultory. Instead I have chosen a line from an ancient poem based on a metaphor that appears in classical Japanese literature to suggest life's fleeting insubstantiality. The actual phrase "bridge of dreams" does not figure in the book any more than does the word "Sarashina"; but dreams, we have seen, recur throughout *Sarashina Nikki*, and the conception of life as a flimsy, dreamlike structure which we cross in our journey from one state of existence to another is central to its theme, just as it is to the last part of *The Tale of Genji*, whose title is taken from this beautiful image.

Only once does Lady Sarashina mention her book itself; and in this passage she gives no clue about when or how it was composed. The consensus among scholars is that she wrote most of it long after the events described, probably during the final years that followed her husband's death. This explains the factual inaccuracies, especially in the early parts, and also helps to account for the literary unity of her work. At various times of her life, though probably not during her girlhood, Lady Sarashina must have made notes of the "pillow book" variety, and she would obviously have referred to them when writing her book; it is almost certain that, just as she recorded her precious dreams, she made copies of all the more interesting poems she sent and received—and also, unfortunately, many of the dull ones.

Sarashina Nikki contains almost a hundred poems, of which three-quarters were written by Lady Sarashina herself. So prominent is this poetry that one famous seventeenth-century authority actually entitled the book *The Sarashina Collection of Verse*. For many Western readers the poems are bound to seem an annoying intrusion: banal, repetitive, and often pointless. In fact, verse plays an essential part, not only in this book, but in all Japanese literature of the Heian period which, to a large extent, derives from the lyric tradition. In the *monogatari* (tales) and *nikki* (diaries) and even in a work like *The Pillow Book* poems are no extraneous embellishment but a natural continuation of the prose text; very often, indeed, they are the sole purpose of that text. One of the most representative genres in early classical literature is the poetry collection, in which a series of poems by the same writer are placed together, often with brief prose introductions explaining the circumstances in which they were composed ("On a clear snowy night in the Eleventh Month the Prince went on a moon-viewing expedition to the Eastern Hills. One of his attendants played the flute. Much moved by the beauty of the scene, His Excellency and his companions exchanged these poems: Like the moon that hovers on those Eastern Hills . . ."). Subsequently the prose passages grew longer and more elaborate, the poems themselves becoming subsidiary to the flow of the narrative and to the development of character. Yet they always remained vital to the conception of the work, even in a huge psychological novel like *The Tale of Genji*, where the emotional climax of a scene will almost invariably be marked by poems like the coda in a musical composition. Throughout the history of Japanese literature until modern times prose and poetry have always been far closer than in the West; in Nō drama, puppet plays, travel journals, and the other typically Japanese genres poetry is as essential as music in a Western religious service.

The integral role of poetry is evident in Lady Sarashina's book. Many sections like 23 to 27 and 31 to 34 consist simply of poems or exchanges of poems with perfunctory prose passages to provide the setting; and poems regularly occur at times of heightened emotion, for instance after her sister's death, almost as if mere prose were unable to bear the weight.

Apart from these literary considerations, poetry pervades *Sarashina Nikki* and the other prose works of the time for the simple reason that it was central to the daily life of the Heian upper classes. The origin of poetry exchanges has been traced to popular gatherings known as "song fences," mentioned in the ancient chronicles, when young men and women engaged in dancing and poetic repartee of an amorous nature; during the Heian period writing and answering poems became as inseparable a part of everyday social life as the telephone for the modern city-dweller. It was the basic form of elegant communication and was crucial in all relations between the sexes, both casual affairs and those that led to marriage; for poetry, as the famous tenth-century writer Ki no Tsurayuki remarked, "softens the relations between men and women." No urbane dweller of Heian Kyō was likely to get through the day without writing and receiving at least a few poems; and even if he escaped to some mountain temple he was expected to send his friends letters with at least one poem a piece, in which the cry of the deer and the booming of the temple bell were almost bound to figure, and to return in due course with several new poems in his notebook. For all her peculiarities Lady Sarashina was in this respect very much a woman of the times. She wrote and received a great deal of poetry, and much of it naturally found its way into her book. Often it is occasional verse of humdrum quality. Convention often obliged people to write poems when they were not in the mood; and of course not all the good people of Heian were blessed with poetic talent throughout their lives. Most of the thousands of poems that the messengers carried from house to house in the Capital must have been of jaw-racking tedium; the tiny fraction that has come down to us represents the best, yet much of it is painfully banal.

On the whole Lady Sarashina's own poems are of high quality (though not in the same class as Ono no Komachi's or Izumi Shikibu's), and many of them were included in later anthologies. This quality will not, I fear, be apparent from my attempts at translation. One of the main difficulties is the deliberate ambiguity of the thirty-one syllable Japanese *uta*. Often two or more entirely different meanings are packed into the same poem (as, for example, on page 68); one interpretation by no means precludes the other; but it is virtually impossible to express them all in English while still retaining some semblance of sense and rhythm. Such ambiguity is by no means peculiar to Japanese poetry; but because of the thirty-one syllable limitation the need to suggest as many meanings as possible in each word and phrase is probably greater than in other literatures. Japanese poets also make great use of word-plays and other stylistic devices that are the despair of any translator. The peculiar resistance of Japanese classical poetry to translation has been summed up by Arthur Waley:

It is not possible that the rest of the world will ever realize the importance of Japanese poetry, because of all poetries it is the most completely untranslatable. Its beauty consists in the perfection with which a thought and a body of sound are fitted into a small rigid frame. An *uta* runs into its mould like quicksilver into a groove. In translation, only the thought survives; the poem no longer 'goes,' any more than a watch goes if you take its works out of their casing and empty them upon a sheet of paper. In the few examples that I am about to give, the reader must for himself discover the *possibility* of poetry. If he is a poet, this will present no difficulty; just as a watch-maker would see in the scattered springs and wheels the possibility of a watch.

27

Waley was a most talented poet; yet, because of the inherent difficulties, his translations of Japanese poetry do not approach even his least successful versions from the Chinese. Probably the best solution is simply to avoid translating *uta;* when it is essential, as in prose works that contain poems, the translator must simply do his best, assuring the reader that they sound quite different in the original and hoping that he will find at least "the possibility of a watch."

The same applies, though perhaps less hopelessly, to the translation in general. Lady Sarashina's prose is remarkably beautiful, far more so, I think, than her highly praised verse; but any attempt to suggest this beauty by reproducing the characteristics of her style in English would be disastrous. The sentences are often extremely long (some of them continuing for three or four pages in Japanese, outdoing even Marcel Proust); but they flow along smoothly without giving the least sense of weight or complexity, so that one feels one is watching a magnificent scroll being slowly unrolled.

Since one of the main points of *Sarashina Nikki* is its style and since no two forms of literary expression could be more different than classical Japanese and modern English, I have deliberately taken liberties with the text so that the English reader may have some intimation of its beauty; but I have never knowingly changed the meaning or added anything that is not in the original. Several years ago a pair of translators, one American and one Japanese, produced an English version entitled *The Sarashina Diary.* Many important works of Japanese literature still remain to be translated, and one tends to avoid books that have already been done. But the 1935 version is so awful that any reader who came across it without any previous knowledge would be tempted to give a miss, not only to *Sarashina Nikki*, but to Japanese literature in general. Apart from being ludicrously inaccurate, it is larded with a succession of quaint exotica that belong to no place and no time, making the "translation" a travesty of Lady Sarashina's clear, idiomatic original. To detail the weaknesses one has found in earlier versions is an easy sport—and also a rather risky one for anyone about to launch his own. Here, however, are a few of the hundreds of atrocities perpetrated on *Sarashina Nikki* when the "inscrutable Orient" approach was still accepted:

'T was the moon-hidden of the Gods-absent month when I went there again for temporary residence. The thick grown leaves which had cast a dark shade were all fallen. The sight was heartfelt all over.

It was a smile-presenting sight. It give a feeling of loneliness to see the dark shadow of the mountain close before me.

On the moon-birth of the Rice-Sprout month I saw the white petals of the Tachibana tree [a kind of orange] near the house covering the ground.

And the prize item:

If I had not given myself up to idle fictions [she herself had written several] and poetry, but had practised religious austerities night and day, I would not have seen such a dream-world . . . Only the sorrowful reflection in the mirror was realized unaltered. O pitiful and sorrowful I!

These examples may be sufficient to explain why I do not regard a new translation of *Sarashina Nikki* as otiose. It has been one of the Japanese books that has given me the greatest pleasure of all, belonging to the category that Waley had in mind when he wrote, "What matters is that a translator should have been excited by the work he translates, should be haunted day and night by the feeling that he *must* put it into his own language, and should be in a state of restlessness and fret till he has done so." In its short ambit *Sarashina Nikki* not only reveals much that is most appealing in the Japanese tradition but stands on its own as an honest, very human picture of a woman.

My main texts have been *Sarashina Nikki Hyōshaku* by Miyata Kazuichirō (Kyoto, 1931) and the Koten Bungaku Taikei edition by Nishishita Kyōichi (Tokyo, 1964). Both these texts, and all the other modern versions of Lady Sarashina's book, are based on the holograph in the hand of the great poet-scholar, Fujiwara no Teika, which is preserved in the archives of the Imperial Household. Even Teika's text has a number of dubious points, as he himself admits in his colophon. It was not produced until about 1230, some two centuries after Lady Sarashina finished her book, and there must be many discrepancies between his version and what she actually wrote. Closer than this, however, we shall never come, except in the unlikely event that an even earlier manuscript turns up in some obscure Kyoto temple.

Lady Sarashina's book has a bizarre textual history. The details are still not entirely clear, but it appears that early in the seventeenth century the threads used in sewing together Fujiwara no Teika's ancient holograph manuscript had worn out and that the pages were taken apart so that they could be securely rebound. The anonymous scholar or binder responsible for this work did a remarkably poor job; for when the pages were sewn together again their order had been changed in no less than seven places, with the result that parts of the book were now virtually meaningless. Yet it was this garbled version that became the basis of all subsequent texts from copies of the manuscript produced in the seventeenth century until modern printed editions three hundred years later.

During the eighteenth century, the great period for the rediscovery of classical Japanese literature and for systematic textual research, Lady Sarashina's book was read by Kamo Mabuchi, Motoori Norinaga, and other scholars of the National Learning Movement. It was recognized, however, that the work was badly flawed by textual confusions. In addition Motoori, the most eminent of these classical scholars, declared that its literary style was inferior to certain earlier works of the Heian period and implied that the book was hardly worth the effort of textual collation that would be necessary to understand it properly. The following desultory conversation between Motoori and one of his disciples, a certain Mr. Tanaka, took place in 1780 and gives a good idea of what scholars knew and thought about Lady Sarashina's book:

TANAKA: If you happen to have a copy of *Sarashina no Nikki* with glosses, I should very much like to borrow it.

MOTOORI: I have no such copy. But since you ask me I shall see if I can get one from a colleague. Of course even this won't have comparisons between the different texts.

TANAKA: The copy I have in there [in my library] is the 1704 edition bound in four books and printed on rice paper . . .

MOTOORI: That is the same as my edition. I doubt whether there are any other printed versions in existence. I vaguely recall that the book I saw last year in Kyoto was a hand-written copy [of the original Teika manuscript].

TANAKA: I wonder whether there isn't some other printed version.[1] By the way, it doesn't say why the book was called *Sarashina*. And a further point: parts of the book are far easier to understand than *Ochikubo Monogatari* and *Kagerō Nikki*;[2] yet I find it very hard to grasp the meaning of certain other parts.

MOTOORI: No, there is no indication why it was given the title *Sarashina*. Probably it refers to the author's state of mind [after her husband died as expressed in] the poem about Mount Obasute at the end of the book.

TANAKA: It appears that she was the daughter of a governor of Shimōsa. She was evidently born in Kyoto, accompanied her father to

---

[1] In fact there were several. The first wood-block edition, the *Fusō Shūyōshū Hon*, was printed in 1693.
[2] Famous tenth-century works of fiction and *belles-lettres* respectively. For details see Index and Glossary of *The World of The Shining Prince* (New York: Alfred A. Knopf, Inc.; London: Oxford University Press, 1964).

his province, and then returned with him to the Capital at the end of his term.

MOTOORI: Not so. It wasn't Shimōsa; it was Hitachi. Her father was appointed to be Assistant Governor of Hitachi and it must have been at this time [that she accompanied him to the provinces] . . .

TANAKA: In any case she went to the Capital and took service at Court as an Imperial Concubine or some such rank. But she seems to have left Court quite often to make pilgrimages to Ishiyama, Hase, and other temples.

MOTOORI: It is true that she served at Court, but it was a very free sort of service. Evidently she just came to Court from time to time. And towards the end it appears that she acquired a husband . . . In sum this book is nothing but a vague, rambling account of her life and it has no central point. It is in the same category as books like *Kagerō* and *Izumi Shikibu Monogatari*.[3] And, since it was written later than *Ochikubo* and *Kagerō*, it is also inferior in style.[4]

By no means the least illuminating part of the conversation between these two eighteenth-century savants is their disagreement about Lady Sarashina's father. Mr. Tanaka opines that he was Governor of Shimōsa, but Motoori tartly contradicts him, pointing out that he was actually Assistant Governor of Hitachi. They are both wrong. As any educated Japanese school child would know, the province where Takasue took his family and served as Governor was neither Shimōsa nor Hitachi, but Kazusa. The conversation between Motoori and his disciple suggests that neither gentleman had read the book very carefully and that Motoori in particular had missed its point.

Though the title and general contents of *Sarashina Nikki* were known by scholars of the National Learning Movement, it

---

[3] Tenth-century feminine works of an autobiographical nature (see Index and Glossary of *The World of The Shining Prince*).

[4] Quoted in Hisamatsu Senichi et al., ed., *Heian Nikki* (Tokyo: 1960), pp. 393–94.

received scant attention compared to the other Heian classics. The reason is not far to seek: parts of the books were so jumbled as to be almost incomprehensible, and besides, the great Motoori had dismissed it as having "no central point."

The same difficulty impeded readers during the nineteenth and early twentieth centuries. It was then realized that several parts of the book were out of order, but the origins of the confusion were unclear and efforts to correct it only made things worse. In the 1890 Nihon Bungaku Zensho version, for example, the editors carefully rearranged some of the early sections of the book where Lady Sarashina's ignorance of geography made it seem that sentences were out of order. As we can now surmise, these mistakes existed in the original manuscript, and by changing them the editors were simply compounding the confusion.

The crucial discovery about what had happened to jumble the sections of Lady Sarashina's book was finally made in 1924 by Professor Tamai, an authority on Heian literature, who describes the momentous event as follows:

It was 1st August, a day I shall never forget. Early in the morning I was taken to the Ministry of the Imperial Household by Dr. [Sasaki] and followed him into . . . Hōmei Hall . . . where a number of treasures had been laid on a table. From among them the assistant in charge took out a box containing the manuscript of *Sarashina Nikki* in the hand of Lord Teika. The outer box, the silk wrapper, the middle box, and the book pouch were removed one by one until finally I saw the precious little [inner] box decorated with a pattern of blue waves and with a moon embossed in lacquer. This too was opened and there lay the book,[5] its cover still dyed in the ancient colours that had lasted for seven hundred years. Just then a faint breeze blew through the window and the splendid fragrance of the old paper was wafted towards me.

---

[5] *Gyohon*, the Imperial Book, so called because it was the property of the Imperial Household.

Dr. [Sasaki] and I started to examine the book . . . and presently in the seam of the binding I detected the first of the clues that I had expected to find as an explanation for the misplacement of the sections. Ah, so the origin of all the confusion really lay in this manuscript! I felt my heart pounding. For some time I had been wondering whether the disorder of the sections was not the result of some carelessness at the time when the manuscript was being re-bound. Now I had the proof before my eyes . . .[6]

By minutely examining the way in which the manuscript had been put together by the seventeenth-century bungler, Professor Tamai was able to identify seven major errors[7] and to reconstruct the book as Teika had originally copied it. Professor Tamai's meticulous work during the following years is the basis of all present texts of *Sarashina Nikki*. His rearrangement of the middle sections has enabled modern readers to understand and enjoy Lady Sarashina's book in a way that was impossible during the preceding centuries. and it has led to a completely new evaluation. "What a blessed event it was for the world of scholarship," writes Dr. Miyata, the editor of the edition on which I have mainly based my translation, "that in the year 1924 the clouds of doubt [about the correct order] which had hung over the text for so many centuries should finally have been swept away and that it could thus be restored to its ancient form!" As it happens, the parts of the book that are mainly read by Japanese school children (still the most numerous audience for works of this kind) are the record of the journey from Kazusa to Kyoto, the account of Lady Sarashina's hunt for *The Tale of Genji*, and the Mount Obasute section, none of which were ever out of order.

Fujiwara no Teika's manuscript, of which I have consulted a

---

[6] *Op. cit.*, pp. 401–02.

[7] These "seven errors in the order of the text" (*sakkan nanakasho*) all occur in the sections that describe the period from 1021 to 1042.

copy produced in 1925, is in free, flowing calligraphy but fairly easy to decipher if one has mastered the Heian style of grass writing and certain archaic forms of the phonetic *hiragana* syllabary. As in all "women's" writing Chinese characters are used sparingly and inconsistently; on the first page, for example, the word *monogatari* (Tale) is written twice with the Chinese character for *mono* ("thing") followed by the phonetic syllables *ka-ta-ri*, and once with only phonetic syllables (*mo-no-ka-ta-ri*). The modern printed texts make no alteration in the actual wording of the original but reduce the effect of such inconsistencies by inserting Chinese characters next to the phonetic symbols of all common words like *monogatari*. When there are obvious errors in the Teika text (Shimotsu*ke* instead of Shimotsu*sa*, for example), the editors insert the necessary corrections in small print beside the original mistaken forms. It is rather as if in a text of Caxton modern English spellings were placed next to the words that are spelled inconsistently in the original. The main textual contribution of Japanese editors is to provide punctuation, which is entirely lacking in the original Heian Japanese. Editors frequently disagree on their punctuation, and from a Westerner's point of view they all tend to over-punctuate; but this rarely causes any trouble. The main difficulties arise from the structure of the sentences themselves, and from the deliberate imprecision of classical Japanese as reflected in the scarcity of pronouns and other forms that are essential in Western writing.

I have followed the order of the book as reconstructed by Professor Tamai. The division into sections and their titles, however, are entirely my own, since all the existing arrangements I have seen, including Professor Miyata's more elaborate system, seemed unsatisfactory and sometimes misleading; the original Teika text, of course, contains no such numbered sections. I have omitted the colophon from my translation; it has scant interest for anyone but the specialist, and he can presumably savour it in the original Sino-Japanese. This colophon first informs us that the author is "the daughter of Sugawara no Takasue, the Governor of Hitachi, her mother being the daughter of Lord Tomoyasu and her aunt being the mother of Fujiwara no Michitsuna." Later come formal biographies of Takasue, Tachibana no Toshimichi (Lady Sarashina's husband), and Minamoto no Sukemichi (the man who might have become her lover). Of Sukemichi, for instance, we are told,

Lord Minamoto no Sukemichi was the first son of Narimasa, Senior Fourth Rank (Upper Grade) who was posthumously appointed to the Junior Third Rank. Having served as Master of the Office of Palace Repairs, he was appointed on the second day of the First Month in the year 1017 to be Assistant Master of the Palace Table, this post being the equivalent [in perquisites] to the two combined shares of the Annual Office accruing to his grandfather, the Major Counsellor . . .

Such particulars, though important for people at the time, are unlikely to rivet the attention of most Western readers. Finally, after a couple of quotations about the coming-of-age ceremony of the High Priestess at Ise, we find a postscript by Fujiwara no Teika explaining the rather chaotic circumstances in which he edited Lady Sarashina's book:

Last year I was able to transmit these notes [i.e., his text of *Sarashina Nikki*], but someone borrowed the book and lost it. Accordingly I once more committed the book to writing, using a copy that someone had made from the copy that was lost. This process of producing a copied edition from another copied edition gave rise to many mistakes. I have placed red marks next to the dubious passages. If a good, accurate text ever comes to hand, it should be compared with my present version and the necessary corrections should be made . . .

We also know from Teika that numerous illustrated versions of *Sarashina Nikki* were available in the thirteenth century. Unfortunately they are among the innumerable casualties of Japan's long civil wars. The illustrations that I have used in this edition are from a wood-block print edition produced in 1704. Though no great works of art in their own right, they are pleasant enough and suggest how people dressed, lived, and travelled in Lady Sarashina's time. I have also included some modern photographs of Lady Sarashina's favourite temples, so that readers who have not had the pleasure of visiting Kyoto and its environs may see the places where she spent so much of her time.

Since this book is designed for the so-called general reader, I have usually omitted from my notes the textual detail, literal versions, and extensive quotations of Japanese sources that accompanied my translation of Sei Shōnagon's *Pillow Book*. To save space I have made frequent cross-references to the second volume of this work and also to *The World of the Shining Prince*, my general study of Heian life. I have included a fairly detailed chronology, based mainly on the one prepared by Professor Miyata in 1931. The dates are all given according to the lunar calendar, in which the full moon invariably came on the fifteenth; this was on an average about one month in advance of our Western calendar so that, for example, the thirteenth day of the Fourth Month in 1042 (Chōkyō III), when Lady Sarashina accompanied the Princess to the Imperial Palace and secretly visited the Sacred Mirror Room, was May 5th, 1042 in the West, the very day on which Edward the Confessor was elected King of England. I have also appended three maps, which were drawn for me by Mrs. Nanae Momiyama, the eminent *sumie* artist, and which show almost all the places mentioned by Lady Sarashina. I am most grateful to Mr. Hōji Shimanaka, the President of the Chūō Kōron Publishing Company, for obtaining illustrations from the 1704 edition of Lady Sarashina's book; to Miss Karen Kennerly, my editor, for all her encouragement and suggestions; to Mr. Shōsuke Takemura and Professor Takeji Iwamiya for their photographs of temples; and to Professor Bunei Tsunoda, Director of the Heian Museum of Ancient History, for checking my maps and for showing me exactly where Lady Sarashina lived in Kyoto one thousand years ago.

Ivan Morris
Kyoto
January 1970

AS I CROSSED
A BRIDGE OF DREAMS

Recollections of a Woman in Eleventh-Century Japan

In my impatience I got a
statue of the Healing Buddha
built in my own size. (p. 41)

1

I was brought up in a part of the country so remote that it lies beyond the end of the Great East Road. What an uncouth creature I must have been in those days! Yet even shut away in the provinces I somehow came to hear that the world contained things known as Tales, and from that moment my greatest desire was to read them for myself. To idle away the time, my sister, my stepmother, and others in the household would tell me stories from the Tales, including episodes about Genji, the Shining Prince; but, since they had to depend on their memories, they could not possibly tell me all I wanted to know and their stories only made me more curious than ever. In my impatience I got a statue of the Healing Buddha built in my own size. When no one was watching, I would perform my ablutions and, stealing into the altar room, would prostrate myself and pray fervently, "Oh, please arrange things so that we may soon go to the Capital, where there are so many Tales, and please let me read them all."

2

On the third day of the Ninth Month, when I was twelve years old, we left our house and moved to a place called Imatachi in preparation for our journey to the Capital. The house where I had played for so many years was dismantled and one could see into the rooms from outside. Everything was in great disorder. As I stepped into the carriage to leave for the last time, the sun had just set and the sky was shrouded with mist. Looking into the house, I caught sight of the Healing Buddha standing there alone —that Buddha before Whom I had prayed so often in secret. At the thought of abandoning Him I began weeping quietly.

The temporary house in Imatachi was a simple place with a thatched roof; in the absence of a proper fence and latticed shutters, our servants had hung up some blinds and curtains. To the south was a wide plain; the sea was close on both sides, and in the evening a beautiful mist covered the entire landscape. I found it so charming that I got up early in the morning and gazed about, thinking how sad it would be to leave this place even though we had been here for only a few days.

We left on the fifteenth, a dark, wet day, and, having crossed the border, lodged at a place called Ikata in the province of Shi-
6 mōsa. It was raining so hard that our cottage was almost afloat, and I was far too frightened to sleep. Looking out, I saw a hillock rising from a bare plain, and on it grew three isolated trees. We spent the next day drying our things that had got soaked and waiting for the other members of the party to catch up with us.

On the seventeenth we set off early in the morning. As we were being ferried across a deep river, one of the boatmen told us that this was the site of a mansion belonging to the Chieftain
7 of Mano, whose workmen used to weave thousands upon thousands of rolls of cloth and then bleach them in these waters. The four great pillars that stood in the river were said to be his ancient gateposts. Some members of our party composed poems for the occasion and I made up this one for myself,

> *Had not the gateposts in the river thus stood firm*
> *But crumbled with the years,*
8   *What trace would now remain to tell me of the past?*

That evening we stayed in Kuroto Beach, where the white dunes stretched out far in the distance. A bright moon hung over the dense pine groves, and the wind soughed forlornly in the branches. The scene inspired us to write poems. Mine was,

> *Had I not stayed awake this night,*
> *When should I have seen the moon—*
> *This Autumn moon that lights Kuroto Beach?*

We left early in the morning and by nightfall had reached

Kagami Rapids on Futoi River, the border between Shimōsa
and Musashi. We stayed at Matsusato Ford, while our men spent
the entire night ferrying our luggage to the other side of the river.

It was here at the provincial border that my nurse, whose
husband had recently died, gave birth to her baby. This meant that
she could no longer travel to the Capital in our company. I was
longing for her that night, and so my elder brother carried me in
his arms to the hut where she lay. Our own lodging was a make-
shift place, but at least it had blinds and hangings to protect us
from the wind. My nurse, having no husband, had been lodged
in a rough, primitive hut. The roof was merely a piece of rush
matting and through it shone the moon, lighting up every corner
of the room. I could read the suffering in her face as she lay there,
so white and pure, covered with a dress of crimson cloth and looking completely transparent in the moonlight. She had not seen me
for some time and began weeping as she stroked my hair. I found
it hard to abandon her there, but my brother was in a hurry to
take me back. On our return I was utterly wretched; her face, still
vivid in my memory, made me so sad that even the sight of the
moon could not console me and I went to bed wilted with sorrow.

On the following morning our carriages were ferried to the
other side of the river and we, too, went across. Now the people
who had accompanied us on the first part of our journey made
their farewells and returned to the east, while those of us who
were continuing to the Capital stayed for a while by the river. At
this parting of the ways we all wept bitterly, and even my childish
heart was full of grief.

We were in Musashi, a province without a single charming
place to recommend it. On the beach the sand was not white but a
sort of muddy colour; in the fields, there were none of the *murasaki* plants I had heard about, but just a mass of reeds growing so
high that even the tips of our horsemen's bows were invisible.
Making our way through the reeds, we reached a temple called

Our carriages were ferried
to the other side of the
river. (p. 43)

Takeshiba. In the distance were the foundation stones of the old   *13*
manor house of the Haha Estate, now a pile of ruins. I asked   *14*
about the place and was told the following story:

"Long ago there was a man of this province with the family
name of Takeshiba. The Governor presented him to the Imperial   *15*
Palace as a guard of watchfires in the fire huts. One day when he   *16*
was sweeping in the Imperial gardens he chanted to himself, 'Why,
oh why have I come to this? At home in my province I have many
a jar of wine, and over the jars hang the gourd ladles. They turn to
the north when the south wind blows, they turn to the south
when the north wind blows, they turn to the east when the west
wind blows, they turn to the west when the east wind blows.
But now I can see none of it.'   *17*

"The Emperor's favourite daughter, standing by the outer
blinds of her Palace leaned against a pillar and gazed at the man.
It moved her that he should be singing there by himself, and she
was curious about those gourd ladles and how they turned above
the jars. Pushing up the blinds, she called, 'Come here, my man!'

"The guard bowed respectfully and hurried to the edge of
the veranda.

" 'Let me hear that song of yours again!' she said, and he repeated it for her. 'Take me there and let me see for myself!' she
told him. 'This is no idle request.'   *18*

"The man was awestruck but, realizing that the Princess had
good reason for her words, he lifted her on his back and set off
for Musashi. Since people were bound to give chase, he stopped
as they were crossing the Bridge of Seta and set the Princess down.   *19*
He destroyed a section of the bridge and leapt across the gap.
Having seated the Princess on his back again, he walked for seven
days and nights until they reached Musashi.

"When they were told about their daughter's disappearance,
the Emperor and Empress were distraught and looked for her
everywhere. Eventually they were informed that a guard had

been seen rushing from the Palace with a creature of great fragrance clinging to his neck. A search was ordered and, presuming that he had returned to his province, they sent Imperial messengers in urgent pursuit. Having reached the Bridge of Seta, the messengers found that it had been damaged and were unable to continue the chase.

"It took them three months before they finally tracked down the man in Musashi Province. The Princess summoned the Imperial messengers and said, 'What I did must have been fated. I was curious about this man's house and told him to bring me here, and so he brought me. And I have found this an excellent place to live in. If the man is punished for this deed, what will become of me? It is no doubt a karma from some previous existence that has made me leave my traces in this province. Go back to the Capital and report this to the Emperor!'

"Unable to argue with the Princess, the messengers returned and told the Emperor what they had heard. 'There is nothing further to be said,' declared His Majesty. 'Even if we punish the man, we can no longer bring our daughter back to the Capital. Of course we can never give him the province of Musashi or entrust him with any official business. But I can unconditionally grant the province to the Princess herself.'

"So the Emperor ordered that a residence be built for them in Musashi in the style of the Imperial Palace, and, when the Princess died, this house became the temple called Takeshiba. Her children were given the family name of Musashi. After that only women were appointed to guard the fire huts."

After crossing hills and fields, which were a desolate waste of reeds, we finally reached Sumida River on the border of Musashi and Sagami. This is the river that appears in Narihira's collection and where he wrote, "Tell me one thing!" We crossed by boat to the province of Sagami.

The range of hills known as Nishitomi was like a row of

folding screens decorated with beautiful paintings. I was charmed by the beach where the great waves beat down and drew away. For several days we walked along the pure white sand of Morokoshi Plain.* I heard someone say that in the summer this plain *27* was covered with Japanese carnations of all shades and looked like a great expanse of brocade; but now it was late autumn and not a single carnation was in bloom, though here and there I noticed some pathetic-looking flowers that had lost their petals. It seemed funny to us that a "Chinese" plain should be famous for its "Japanese" carnations.

Mount Ashigara, which is about ten miles across, is covered *28* with a terrifyingly dark wood; from the moment we entered the mountain forest at the base we could catch only an occasional glimpse of the sky. We lodged at the foot of the mountain, and I felt fearfully lost in the depth of the moonless night. From somewhere in the dark three women singers emerged, the eldest being *29* about fifty, the others about twenty and fourteen. They set up a large umbrella in front of our hut, and our servants lit a fire. The oldest woman told us that she was the granddaughter of the famous singer, Kohata. Their hair, which was extremely long, hung beautifully over their foreheads; they all had fair complexions and looked attractive enough to serve as waiting-women.

Our party was charmed by their appearance and even more impressed when they started singing, for they had fine, clear voices that rose to the heavens. The women were invited to join us. One member of our group remarked that the singers in the western provinces were no match for these performers, whereupon they burst out into a splendid song, "Should you compare us with those of Naniwa . . ." Yes, they were really pretty to look at, and their *30* beautiful singing ended far too soon. We were all so sad to see them disappear into those fearful mountains that we wept as they

---

*Lit. "Plain of China."

walked away. I, being young and impressionable, was particularly moved by the scene and, when the time came, did not want to leave the shelter of our hut.

We crossed Mount Ashigara at dawn. If even the bottom of the mountain could scare me, how much more terrifying it became as we made our way into the depths of the forest, going higher and higher until we were stepping on the very clouds! About halfway to the top the trees became sparser and we came to a place where nothing grew but three *aoi* plants. It was touching to see them standing there by themselves on this remote mountain slope. There were also three streams flowing down the mountain.

At length we reached the other side of Ashigara and stopped at the barrier mountain on the border of Suruga Province. Here we visited Iwatsubo,* where there was a fantastically large square rock. From a hole in the rock gushed water as pure and cool as any I had ever tasted.

In Suruga stands Mount Fuji, which I used to see in the West from the province where I grew up. There is no mountain like it in the world. It has a most unusual shape and seems to have been painted deep blue; its thick cover of unmelting snow gives the impression that the mountain is wearing a white jacket over a dress of deep violet. At the summit is a level place from which smoke emerges, and in the evening we actually saw a fire burning there.

We reached Kiyomi Barrier by the sea. On the beach were some huts belonging to the barrier keepers, and the palisades went all the way down to the water. The spray from the huge waves mingled beautifully with the smoke from the keepers' huts.

At Tagonoura also the waves were high and we were rowed round the bay.

31

32

33

34

48

*Lit. "Rock Bowl."

In Suruga stands Mount
Fuji. (p. 48)

35   When we came to the ford in Ōi River, I was astounded by the torrent of water, which rushed along like a thick white stream of powdered rice.

Next we reached Fuji River, whose source is in Mount Fuji. A man of Suruga joined us and told the following story:

"Once when I was going on a pilgrimage, I stopped by this river to rest from the heat. As I sat here, I noticed a yellow object floating downstream. Presently it caught on something, and I was able to pick it up. It turned out to be a scrap of paper on which were written many characters in heavy red ink. 'Very odd!' thought I and decided to have a good look. The words on the paper were the names of the provincial governors who were to be included
36   in the List of Appointments for the following year, all set down properly like an official list. Our own Governor's term was coming to an end, and there was the name of the new Governor with another name beside it. Amazed at my discovery, I carefully dried the paper and put it away. When the appointments were announced in the following year, they were all exactly as announced on that piece of paper. The gentleman who had been named as our new governor was duly appointed, but he died after three months and his successor was the other man. Yes, such things happen in this world of ours. They say that the Gods gather on this mountain to decide matters like next year's appointments. Strange, isn't it?"

Everything went well until we passed Numajiri. There I fell ill, and by the time we reached the province of Tōtōmi I was in such a state that I cannot even remember crossing the mountain
37   pass at Saya no Nakayama. On reaching Tenchū River the men
38   built a temporary hut for me where I spent a few days while recovering.

The winter was now advanced and fierce winds flew from
39   the river. We crossed and made our way to Hamana. When we had journeyed in the opposite direction on our way to Kazusa,

there had been a long bridge in this place, but now we could find no trace of it and had to cross by boat. On one side was the ocean with its huge, rough breakers; on the other lay the plain shoals of the lagoon, where through the thick branches of the pine trees we could see the waves sparkling like many-coloured jewels. It was a delightful scene: nothing but the pine forest and the waves, which looked as if they were washing across the tips of the branches. *40*

Leaving Hamana, we had a tiresome climb over the Slope of Inohana and reached Takashi Beach in the province of Mikawa. Next we passed a village called Yatsuhashi,* but it was a dull place and there was no trace of the bridges except in the name. We spent the night on Mount Futamura under a huge persimmon tree. All night the fruit kept falling on the roofs of our huts, and our men went out to collect it.

Though it was already the end of the Tenth Month when *41* we crossed Mount Miyaji, the maple leaves were still at their height. I composed the poem,

So the storms have not yet come to Mount Miyaji!
For russet leaves still peacefully adorn the hills.

I enjoyed seeing the Ford of Shikasuga between the provinces of Mikawa and Owari and was truly worried about whether or not to cross. *42*

When we reached Narumi Bay in the province of Owari, the evening tide was coming in rapidly. This was obviously no place to spend the night since we were in danger of being stranded when the tide came in, and everyone crossed helter-skelter to the other side.

At the border of Mino province we took the ferry at Sunomata and reached a place called Nogami. Here again we were

---

*"Eight Bridges."

joined by a band of entertainers, who sang for us all night long, bringing back fond memories of Mount Ashigara. A wild snowstorm blew up on the following day, and we could not enjoy anything during our crossing of Fuha Barrier and Mount Atsumi.

43 In Ōmi Province we spent a few days in Okinaga's house.

When we came to the foot of Mount Mitsukasa it rained day and night—a cold winter rain mixed with hail. There was not a glimmer of sun and we found it most depressing. Making our way past Inugami, Kamuzaki, Yasu, and Kurumoto, we finally

44 caught sight of the Lake spread out far in the distance with a charming view of Nade, Chikubu, and the other little islands. It was difficult to get across, however, as the Seta Bridge had collapsed.

Having stopped at Awazu, we reached the Capital on the second day of the Twelfth Month. We had planned to enter the city after nightfall and had therefore left Awazu at about five

45 o'clock in the afternoon. As we approached the Barrier, I caught sight of a vast Buddha, rising about sixteen feet behind a simple wooden fence on the edge of the mountain. The statue had not yet been completed, and it was the face alone that I saw looking down on us. "Oh, what a solitary Buddha!" I thought as we went by. "There he stands, far from all human beings, and totally indifferent to his surroundings."

In all the provinces that we had passed the most impressive barriers were Kiyomi in Suruga and this Barrier of Ōsaka. It was

46 dark by the time we reached our house to the west of Sanjō Palace.

3 *1120*

The house was set in rough, uncultivated grounds, over-grown with trees that were as large and frightening as those we had seen in the mountains during our journey. In these wild surroundings it was hard to believe that we were actually back in the Capital.

Now that we had finally arrived, I was desperately impatient to read some Tales. Though our household was still in confusion, I begged my stepmother to help me, and she wrote to our cousin, Lady Emon, who was a lady-in-waiting to the Princess in Sanjō Palace. Lady Emon, surprised and pleased by my request, sent me the lid of an inkbox containing an unusually fine collection of notebooks which, as she explained, had been passed on to her by Her Highness, the Princess. Overjoyed with this gift, I plunged into the Tales and read them day and night. I was eager for more. But who in the Capital was going to help this newcomer in such a quest? *47*

My stepmother, who had served at Court before moving to the provinces, had been going through a difficult time and her marriage was no longer satisfactory. She now decided to leave, taking along her four-year-old child. "You have been very kind," she said to me. "I shall never forget it." Pointing to the great plum tree that grew close to the eaves of our house, she added as her parting words, "When this tree blooms again, I shall be back." After she left I yearned for her and wept silently day after day. And so the year drew to an end. *48*

I kept looking at the plum tree, waiting impatiently for the blossoms to appear and wondering whether she would keep her word. In time the tree flowered, but still there was no word from her. Utterly dejected, I broke off a branch and sent it with the poem,

You promised to return.
How long must I still wait till you fulfil that vow?
Spring did not forget the tree
Whose branches once were white with frost.

She replied affectionately and sent the poem, 53

Do not give up your waiting!
One unawaited and who made no vow
(49) *Will soon, I hear, visit the plum tree's trailing branch.*

During the spring there was a terrible epidemic, and my
50 nurse, on whom I had gazed so tenderly in the moonlight at Matsusato Ford, died on the first day of the Third Month. I was
crushed by grief and even lost my interest in Tales. All day long I
shook with weeping; then I noticed how the evening sun threw
its brilliant light on the scattering blooms of the cherry tree, and I
wrote the poem,

> *They will come back next Spring—those cherry blooms*
> *that scatter from the tree.*
> *But how I yearn for her who left*
> *And never will return!*

At about the same time I heard that the daughter of His
Excellency, the Chamberlain Major Counsellor, had died. Plunged
as I was in my sorrow, I could easily sympathize with her husband,
the Middle Captain. On my arrival in the Capital someone had
51 given me a book of this lady's calligraphy as a model for my own
writing practice. I remembered how she wrote the line, "Had
52 I not lain awake last night," and after this came the poem,

> *When smoke arises from the Field of Toribe,*
53 > *See the last vestiges of one whose life was no less frail!*

The sight of these verses, which she had copied in a hand of re-
markable beauty, brought on a fresh fit of weeping.

Seeing that I had abandoned myself to grief, Mother did her
best to console me and managed to find some more Tales. These
had the expected effect and almost immediately my spirits improved. I read some of the books about Lady Murasaki and longed
54 to see the later parts. Since I was still new to the Capital and had
no one to ask, it was impossible to find what I wanted. I was burn-

ing with impatience and curiosity, and in my prayers I used to say, "Let me see the entire *Tale of Genji* from beginning to end!" When I went with Mother to Uzumasa on a retreat, this was the one thing I prayed for. If only I could find a complete copy which I could start reading as soon as we got home! Yet my prayers were all in vain.

I was feeling most dejected when one day I called on an aunt of mine who had come up from the country. She received me affectionately and showed great interest in me. "What a pretty girl you've grown up to be!" she said. As I was leaving she asked, "What would you like as a present? I am sure you don't want anything too practical. I'd like to give you something you will really enjoy."

And so it was that she presented me with fifty-odd volumes of *The Tale of Genji* in a special case, together with copies of *Zai, Tōgimi, Serikawa, Shirara, Asauzu,* and many other Tales. Oh, how happy I was when I came home with all these books in a bag! In the past I had been able to have only an occasional hurried look at fragments of *The Tale of Genji,* and much of it had remained infuriatingly obscure. Now I had it all in front of me and I could sit undisturbed behind my curtain, bent comfortably forward as I took out the books one by one and enjoyed them to my heart's content. I wouldn't have changed places with the Empress herself.

Placing the lamp close to where I sat, I kept reading all day long and as late as possible into the night. Soon I came to know the names of all the characters in the book and I could see them clearly in my mind's eye, which gave me the greatest satisfaction. One night I dreamt that a handsome priest appeared before me in a yellow surplice and ordered me to learn the fifth volume of the Lotus Sutra as soon as possible. I told no one about the dream, since I was much too busy with my Tales to spend any time learning sutras. I was not a very attractive girl at the time, but I fancied that, when I grew up, I would surely become a great beauty with

55 margin note

56 margin note

57 margin note

I kept reading all day long
and as late as possible into
the night. (p. 55)

long flowing hair like Yūgao, who was loved by the Shining Prince, or like Ukifune, who was wooed by the Captain of Uji. Oh, what futile conceits!

58

At the very beginning of the Fifth Month, as I gazed at the pure white orange blossoms near the eaves of our house, I wrote the poem,

> *It is their scent alone*
> *That tells me what those scattered orange blossoms are.*
> *Else I should have thought they were*
> *Untimely flakes of snow.*

The trees in our garden grew as thickly as those that spread their darkness at the foot of Mount Ashigara, and in the Tenth Month we had a blaze of red leaves, like a rich covering of brocade, which was far more impressive than anything on the surrounding hills. A visitor to our house mentioned that he had passed a place with some magnificent red foliage, and I improvized,

59

> *What can excel this garden where I dwell*
> *In my autumnal weariness?*

60

I continued thinking all day about the Tales, and Tales filled my thoughts every night until I fell asleep. One night I dreamt that a man came to me and said, "I have just finished building a stream in the Hall of Six Sides. It is for the Princess of the First Order, the daughter of the Empress Dowager." When I asked for an explanation, he replied, "Offer prayers to the Heavenly Goddess, Amaterasu!" But his words were wasted on me; I neither told anyone about the dream nor gave it further thought. In the Spring I used to gaze into the garden of this Princess's palace, and one day I composed the poem,

61

62

> *As I long for her cherry trees to bloom*
> *And grieve when her blossoms start to fall,*
> *This seems my own garden into which I gaze.*

1022.iii

Towards the end of the Third Month I moved into a friend's
63 house to escape the Earth God. The cherry trees in the garden were
still in bloom, and when I returned home on the following day I
sent this poem to my hosts,

> *Ah, what joy it was to stay*
> *And gaze at the unending beauty of your blooms,*
> *Soon to be scattered now that Spring has gone!*

Each Spring when the flowers blossomed and were blown away I
was sadly reminded that this was the season when my nurse had
died. Taking out the calligraphy book of the Chamberlain Major
Counsellor's daughter, who had died at the same time, I would
sit there numb with grief and stare intently at her writing.

4

Late one Spring night, while immersed in a Tale, I heard a
prolonged miaow. I looked up with a start and saw an extremely
pretty cat. Where on earth was it from, I wondered. Just then my
sister came behind the curtain. "Hush!" she said. "Not a word to
anyone! It's a darling cat. Let's keep it!"

The cat was very friendly and lay down beside us. Since we
were afraid that people might come looking for her, we kept her
hidden in our part of the house. There she stayed faithfully, cud-
dled up between us; she never went near the servants' quarters and
64 would eat only the daintiest food. We looked after her with great
care until one day my sister fell ill and in the confusion I decided
65 to keep our cat in the northern wing of the house. She miaowed
loudly at not being allowed into our rooms, but I had expected
this and, pitiful though her cries were, I thought it better to keep
her away during my sister's illness.

One day my sister suddenly said, "What's happened?
Where's our cat? Bring her here!"

I looked up with a start and saw an extremely pretty cat. (p. 58)

"Why?" I asked.

"I've had a dream," she explained. "Our cat came to me and said, 'I am the daughter of the Chamberlain Major Counsellor, and it is in this form that I have been reborn. Because of some karma between us, your sister grew very fond of me and so I have stayed in this house for a time. But recently she has put me in the servants' quarters, which I find terrible.' She cried and cried, and I thought she looked like a very beautiful and elegant woman. When I awoke, I realized that the words in my dream were the miaowing of our cat. This dream has moved me deeply." I too was moved by my sister's story and thereafter never sent the cat to the northern wing, but looked after her carefully in my own room.

Once when I was alone she came and sat beside me. I stroked her for a long time. "So you are the Major Counsellor's daughter!" I said. "If only I could let His Excellency know that you are here!" Hearing this, she gazed at me intently and gave a long miaow. It may have been my imagination but at that moment her eyes were not those of an ordinary cat; they seemed to understand exactly what I was saying.

66
67
I heard of a family that owned a copy of *The Song of Everlasting Regret* rewritten as a Tale. I longed to see it, but could not bring myself to ask them. On the seventh day of the Seventh Month I found a suitable opportunity and sent them the poem,

> Long ago the Herdsman and the Weaver made their vow.
> Today my fond thoughts go to them, and yearning waves
>   of Heaven's River surge within my heart.

This was their reply:

> Fondly indeed one views the river where those lovers meet,
> And forgets the sadness of their ill-starred love.

On the thirteenth night of that month the moon shone

brightly, lighting every corner of the earth. At about midnight, when the rest of our household was asleep, my sister and I sat on the veranda. "If I flew away now all of a sudden and disappeared without a trace," she said, gazing at the sky, "what would you think?" Then, seeing the anxious look on my face, she changed the subject and soon she was laughing and chatting merrily. Presently a carriage approached with a forerunner and stopped by our house. The passenger ordered his attendant to call for someone. "Oginoha, Oginoha!"* cried the man, but there was no reply from inside the house and presently he gave up. The gentleman played his flute for a while in a beautiful, clear tone; then the carriage moved away. After it had left I said,

> *That flute was like the Autumn wind.*
> *Why did the Reed Leaf make no gentle answering sound?*

My sister nodded and replied,

> *It was the flute's fault, for it passed too soon*
> *And did not wait for Reed Leaf to reply.*

We sat there all night, looking at the sky; at dawn we went to bed.

In the Fourth Month of the following year there was a fire in our house and the cat whom we had tended so carefully as the daughter of His Excellency the Major Counsellor was burnt to death. Whenever I used to call out "Counsellor's daughter!" this cat had miaowed and come to me with a look of understanding on her face. "It really is extraordinary," Father used to say. "I must tell His Excellency about it." How pathetic that she should have died like this!

---

* "Reed Leaf."

5

We now had to move into a new house. The old one had been a spacious place that gave one the feeling of being deep in the mountains; and our garden with its Spring blossoms and Autumn leaves had far outshone the surrounding hills. The present house, which had a tiny garden and no trees at all, was smaller than anything I had seen, and the move saddened me greatly. The garden opposite was full of plum trees, which blossomed in a profusion of red and white; when there was a breeze, their scent wafted towards me. One day, overcome with memories of the old house to which I had grown so accustomed, I composed the poem,

From the neighbouring garden comes a scented breeze.
Deeply I breathe it in, though longing all the while
For the plum tree by our ancient eaves.

On the first day of the Fifth Month my sister died while giving birth to her baby. Ever since I was a child the news of people's death, even that of strangers, had disturbed me greatly, and it used to take a long time to recover from the shock. How shattering then was the death of my own sister! I simply cannot describe it. While Mother and the others were gathered in the room where she had died, I took the two little children she had left behind and lay down in my own room, putting one child on my left side, the other on my right. As we lay there, the moon shone through the cracks of the broken shingle roof and lit up the face of one of the children. This seemed a bad omen, so I covered the child's face with the sleeve of my robe and drew the other child close to me. It was distressing to think of what the future would bring.

Some days later I received a letter from a relation: "Your sister asked me to get a copy of this book for her, but I simply could not find one. Just now someone happened to send me a copy. How very sad!" With her letter came a Tale entitled *The Princess Who Sought a Corpse.* Sad indeed! I sent this poem in reply,

70

Why should she wish to read of an unburied corpse—
She who now lies beneath the moss?

My sister's old nurse decided there was nothing to keep her
in our house any longer and with much weeping she prepared to
leave us and go home. I sent her the farewell poem,

As she went, so you are leaving too.
Ah, sorrowful indeed these partings!

"If only I could keep you here as a memory of her!" I added.
"I can write no more; for the water in my inkstone has frozen,
and my heart too is blocked with grief."

My brush's strokes that used to flow so free
Have frozen stiff as icicles.
What can I write that will remain
A lasting memory of her who has gone?

Nurse sent this reply,

There is no comfort left for me.
Why should the plover now remain
On the strand of this sad world?   71

After visiting my sister's grave, Nurse returned in tears and I
wrote a further poem,

There in Toribe Field
Even the smoke that rose above the pyre
Has vanished in the sky.
What traces still remained
To lead her to my sister's grave?   72

My stepmother heard about this and sent the following
verse,

There was no trace to lead her to the burial place.
The only guides were tears
That fell before her as she walked.

63

Our relation who had sent a copy of *The Princess Who Sought a Corpse* wrote the poem,

Ah, what cruel grief was hers
As she wandered weeping in that desolate bamboo plain,
Searching for an unmarked grave!

My brother, who had accompanied the funeral procession on that sad night, read this poem and wrote,

That smoke we watched above her pyre
Has vanished utterly.
How can she have hoped to find the grave
Among the bamboo grasses of the plain?

6

73 At a time when it had been snowing for many days I thought of the nun on Mount Yoshino and wrote the poem,

Few travellers pass that way at any time.
Now that the snow has come,
Whom can she hope to see
On Yoshino's steep mountain path?

7 10 24

74 Father had been expecting to celebrate a new appointment after the announcement of the New Year's List, but his hopes were dashed. On the following morning came a letter from someone who had been awaiting the List with the same feelings as ours: "I stayed up all night waiting impatiently for dawn, and confident that my hopes would be realized in spite of everything."

When the tolling of the temple bell
Told me that dawn and my vigil's end had come at last,
I felt as though I'd passed a hundred Autumn nights.

I sent this reply poem,

Why wait the tolling of the temple bell
On a day that took such heavy toll of all our hopes? 75

Towards the end of the Fourth Month I had to move to a house
in the Eastern Hills, and on my way I passed many ricefields. 76
Some of the beds were full of water, while in others the seedlings
had already been planted; and they were all delightfully green.
But, reaching the house itself, which lay directly opposite a hill,
I found it dark and gloomy; in the evening when the waterrails
began their endless tapping I felt depressed and wrote,

Tap, tap though you may, oh water rail,
What visitor will come along the mountain path at this late hour
And knock upon my door? 77

Since the house was near Ryōzen, I and a companion went 78
up there on the following day to say our prayers. After the steep
climb we stopped for a while by the stone well in the temple.
Scooping up the water in our hands, we had a delicious drink. "I
don't think I could ever get enough of this water," remarked my
companion, and I said,

So the water that you've scooped between the stones
In this distant mountain well
Has told you that you'll never have your fill
However much you drink! 79

We stopped for a while by
the stone well. (p. 65)

This was her reply,

No, I shall never drink my fill,
For it is sweeter even than the water of the well
That was muddied by the drops.

On our way down from the temple the evening sun shone brightly and we had a beautiful view of the Capital. My companion who had composed the poem about the muddied water had to leave for the city. The parting saddened me and the next morning I sent her this verse,

The setting sun that hung above the mountain's edge
Has now sunk out of sight.
How sad it was to see you go!

At dawn I was much moved to hear the priests invoking the Sacred Name as they prostrated themselves before the Buddha. I pushed open my door and looked out. The ridges of the mountains shone dimly in the early light, and the tops of the trees that darkly covered the hillside were veiled with mist. These dense trees lent the cloudy sky a special charm that one would not find in blossom time or in the season of red leaves. On a nearby branch a *hototogisu* was singing away. This was my poem,

To whom shall I show it,
To whose ears shall I bring it—
This dawn in the mountain village,
This music of the hototogisu *as he greets another day?*

On the last of the month I heard a *hototogisu* singing loudly in a tree near the valley and I wrote,

The city dwellers still await your voice,
But here, oh hototogisu, *we've heard your singing all day long!*

For some time my companion and I sat silently absorbed in

our thoughts. Then she said, "Do you suppose anyone in the Capital is listening to a *hototogisu* at this very moment, or thinking about us in this village and imagining how we sit here sunk in thought,"

Of all those dwellers in the Capital who gaze upon this moon
How many send their thoughts to us
Who sit here musing in our mountain depths?

I replied with the poem,

Moon-gazers late at night
Are bound to think of mountain villages like ours,
Though no one dwell there whom they know.

82

Once when I awoke at dawn I heard what sounded like a group of people coming down the mountainside. Looking out, I saw that it was a deer who had walked all the way to the veranda and who now stood there crying. The nearby cry of a deer is not a pleasant sound, and I wrote,

The deer's love call to his mate on Autumn nights
Is a thing that one should hear from distant mountain sides.

On learning that a friend had been near the village and had returned to the Capital without telling me, I wrote,

Even the wind that soughs in pine trees on the mountain side
And does not care what people think
Will always make some sign to tell us when it leaves.

83

Late one night towards the end of the Eighth Month I gazed at the wonderful dawn moon illuminating the dark clusters of trees and the mountainside, and I listened to the beautiful sound of the waterfall.

If only I could share this moon
With one whose feelings are like mine—
This moon that lights the mountain village in the Autumn dawn!

68

I saw that it was a deer. (p. 68)

On my way back to the Capital the rice fields, which were covered with water when I went up to the village, had all been harvested, and I wrote,

When I came this way before,
There was nothing in these fields but water for the seedlings' growth.
Now the crop has grown and the harvest's done—
So long have I lingered here.

When I returned to the Eastern Hills for a short while towards the end of the Tenth Month, all the dense foliage had disappeared, and the water that had flowed with such a pleasant rustling sound was buried in dead leaves so that only the water course was visible. Observing this cheerless scene, I wrote,

So barren now these mountain sides,
Where the leaves have scattered in the storms,
That even the rippling stream has vanished from my sight.

"I shall be back next Spring if I am still alive," I said to the nun who lived there. "Please let me know as soon as the flowers are in bloom." Then I returned to the Capital.

In the middle of the Third Month of the following year I had still not heard from the nun, and so I sent this poem,

Still no news of blossom time!
Has Spring not come this year,
Or did the flowers forget to bloom?

9

One bright moonlit night, when I was on a journey and staying in a house by a bamboo grove, I awoke to the sound of the leaves rustling in the wind. As I lay there, unable to go back to sleep, I wrote the poem,

Night after night I lie awake,
Listening to the rustle of the bamboo leaves,
And a strange sadness fills my heart. 84

When I left in the Autumn and moved to another house, I gave this poem to my hosts,

The kindly dew befriends me everywhere,
Yet my fondest thoughts are for your Autumn plain of reeds. 85

10

My former stepmother was still known in Court circles by the name of the province where she had lived with Father when he was Governor; she kept this name even after she acquired a new husband. When Father heard about this, he said he would 86 send word to her that he disapproved. I learnt about the matter and wrote this poem for him,

Oh you, who now have gone to dwell among the clouds, 87
Do you still call yourself by my old name?

11

I lived forever in a dream world. Though I made occasional pilgrimages to temples, I could never bring myself to pray sincerely for what most people want. I know there are many who 88 read the sutras and practise religious devotions from the age of about seventeen; but I had no interest in such things. The height of my aspirations was that a man of noble birth, perfect in both looks and manners, someone like Shining Genji in the Tale, would visit me just once a year in the mountain village where he would have hidden me like Lady Ukifune. There I should live my lonely existence, gazing at the blossoms and the Autumn leaves and the moon and the snow, and wait for an occasional splendid letter from him. This was all I wanted; and in time I came to believe that it would actually happen.

It occurred to me that my position in the world would greatly improve if Father received a proper appointment. I was hoping against hope when finally his new post was announced; but he was assigned to a very distant province.

"All these years" said Father "I have been looking forward to the day—a day that I thought would come soon—when I would be appointed to one of the nearby provinces. Then I should have been able to look after you properly. I could have taken you along to my province and shown you the sea and the mountains and all the other beautiful sights. Above all, I should have made sure that you would get better treatment than the daughter of a mere provincial official. But you and I seem to have had bad karmas. To think that after all this waiting I should now have been sent to such a place! Many years ago when I took you to the East, I used to worry about you whenever I had the slightest illness. For, though you were just a little girl at the time, I knew what a difficult life you would have if I died and left you there in the wilds of Kazusa. The provinces are terrible places. I could have managed if I had only had myself to think about, but it worried me to be accompanied by a large family and to know that I was hemmed in by restrictions of every kind and could not look after you as I wished. Now that you have grown up, things are even more difficult. I may not be long for this world and I can think of all too many examples of girls who have lost their fathers and then gone to seed in the Capital. Your plight will be worse still if I take you along to the East and you turn into a mere country woman. On the other hand, what will happen if you stay behind in the Capital, where we have no relations or connexions to count on? Yet there is no alternative. After all, I can hardly resign my post now that I have finally received this appointment. I suppose I shall simply have to say a last farewell and leave you here. But I know that you will have a hard time managing without me."

Thus he lamented day and night, making me so unhappy that I could no longer even notice the beauty of the flowers and the leaves. Soon I was in a really miserable state, but there was nothing to be done about it.

It was on the thirteenth day of the Seventh Month that Father left for his province. During the five days before his departure he did not visit my room a single time, since our meetings only made things worse. As a result, when the actual day came, we were even more upset than we would have been otherwise.

"The time has come," said Father, raising the blind in my room. We looked at each other and wept bitterly. Then he left without another word. After he had gone, I lay there motionless, and my tears made everything turn dark.

Presently one of Father's servants, who had been ordered to remain in the Capital but who had gone along part of the way to see him off, returned carrying a pocket-paper with the poem, *92*

> *Fate is no friend of mine.*
> *Even this Autumn parting has been marred by haste.* *93*

This was all Father had written, but I could not finish reading it. I had great difficulty in replying. Even at the best of times I was not much good at poetry, and at a moment like this I felt quite *94* incapable of expressing myself. I believe I jotted down something to the effect,

> *I never dreamt that such a thing could be—*
> *That you and I should part in this world even for a while.*

After Father left, we had fewer visitors than ever. I sat forlornly in my room, wondering exactly where he might be. Since

I knew the road to the East, I was able to follow him lovingly in my mind, and from dawn till dusk I gazed sadly at the ridges of the Eastern Hills.

1032. viii

95   In the Eighth Month I made a pilgrimage to Uzumasa. On my way along the First Avenue I saw two carriages that had stopped by the side of the road. The gentlemen inside were evidently waiting for someone who was to accompany them. As my carriage passed, they sent an escort with the message,

96   *Ah, so she's off to view the flowers!*

My companions said it would be improper not to reply, so I simply sent back these lines before continuing on my way,

Now that the Autumn fields are all in bloom,
You who are used to many plants
Are bound to think like this:

During the entire seven days of my retreat my thoughts were constantly of Father's journey to the East. I prayed that somehow he might get rid of his official duties so that we could soon meet safely again. Surely Buddha must have felt some sympathy for me.

Winter came. One night, after a heavy day's rain, a fierce wind blew away the rain clouds so that the moon shone brightly in a clear sky. Noticing that the clover leaves by our eaves had been thoroughly battered by the wind, I was much moved and composed this poem,

How fondly they must think of Autumn days—
These withered clover leaves
97   *That now are lashed by Winter storms!*

A messenger arrived from the East with a letter from Father:
98   "When I was making my circuit of the Shrines, I came to a large plain; a beautiful river flowed through it, and there was also a thick forest. 'What a pretty sight.' I thought, and then immedi-

74

I saw two carriages that had stopped by the side of the road. (p. 74)

ately regretted that I could not show it to you. I asked the name of the place and learnt that the forest was called Child-Yearning —appropriate indeed in my present state of mind. Sadly I got off my horse and stayed there for a long time sunk in thought. These lines occurred to me,"

> Forest of Child-Yearning
> How sad it is to see you here!
> Have you too left your child behind
> That you stay thus sunk in doleful thoughts?

I need hardly say what my own feelings were as I read Father's letter. I sent him this poem by way of reply,

> Yearning for One's Child—
> How bitterly that name recalls the eastern lands
> And Mount Chichibu,* which left its child behind!

12

As I was whiling away the time in gloomy musings, it occurred to me that I might go on some pilgrimages. "How terrifying!" said Mother, who was a very old-fashioned woman. "If we go to Hase, we may be attacked by brigands on Nara Slope and what will become of us then? Ishiyama is also very dangerous because one has to cross the barrier mountain. And Mount Kurama—oh, how that would scare me! You had better wait until your father returns and let him decide where it's safe to go." She obviously regarded me as a great nuisance and unfit for normal society; the most she would allow was a retreat in Kiyomizu. But when we reached the temple I still could not pray sincerely as I should.

---

* *Chichi* means "father."

During the Equinox, when the temple was in a terrible commotion, I dozed off one evening and dreamt that a priest approached me in the curtained enclosure by the altar. This priest, whom I took to be the Intendant of the Temple, wore a vestment with a blue design, a brocade cowl, and a pair of brocaded shoes. "Engaged in senseless trifling," he said, "you are risking your future salvation." Having delivered this scolding, he disappeared behind the curtain and I woke up. I told no one about the dream and left the temple without giving it any further thought.

13 1035
age 27

Mother ordered a one-foot mirror to be made for Hase Temple. Since she was unable to take it there herself, she decided to send a priest in her place and gave him the following instructions, "You are to stay in retreat for three days and you must pray for a dream about my daughter's future." While the priest was away, Mother made me observe strict rules of abstinence.

On his return the priest reported to Mother, "I did not know how to face you if I came back from Hase without a dream. So I prayed devoutly before the altar and performed all my observances with the utmost devotion. Then I went to sleep and dreamt that a most beautiful and noble-looking lady appeared from behind the curtain, dressed in splendid robes. Raising the mirror that you had dedicated to the temple, she asked, 'Has a Statement of Dedication been presented with this mirror?'

" 'No, Madam,' I replied. 'I have no such document. I was simply ordered to present the mirror.'

" 'Very strange!' she said. 'There should have been a statement.' Then she pointed to your mirror. 'Look what is reflected here!' she said and began crying bitterly. 'The sight fills one with grief.' In the mirror I saw a figure rolling on the floor in weep-

I prayed devoutly before
the altar. (p. 78)

ing and lamentation. 'Very sad, is it not?' she said. 'But now look at this!' Then she showed me the other side. There was a dais with fresh green hangings and, from under a curtain of state in the far end of the room, emerged a profusion of sleeves and trains of many-coloured robes; beyond the room one could see the plum blossoms and cherry blossoms in the garden, and the singing warblers were flying from tree to tree. 'This makes one happy, does it not?' said the lady. And that was the end of my dream.''

Though the dream concerned my own future, I paid no attention to it at the time. So indifferent was I to such matters that when I was repeatedly told to pray to the Heavenly Goddess Amaterasu I wondered where this deity might be and whether She was in fact a Goddess or a Buddha. It was some time before I was interested enough to ask who She actually was.

"She is a Goddess," I was told, "and She is enshrined in Ise. It is She who is worshipped by the Provincial Chieftain of Kii, and She is also enshrined as the Guardian Deity of the Sacred Mirror Room.''

Since I could hardly go all the way to Ise to pray to the Heavenly Goddess and since I had no access to the Sacred Mirror Room, it occurred to me that at least I could offer my prayers to the light in heaven.

14

To a relation of mine who had become a nun in Shugaku Temple I sent the following poem in Winter,

> *My thoughts go out to you*
> *In your wintry mountain home,*
> *And, picturing the storms that rage about your head,*
> *I find myself in tears.*

This was her reply,

How good you are to send those thoughts to one
Who wanders in a state of mind as drear
As the dense, dark groves of summer trees!   *109*

Father finally returned from the East, and we moved into a house
in the Western Hills. We stayed up all night, happily exchanging   *110*
stories, and I composed the poem,

Who could have thought that such great joy would come?
How sad that Autumn when you left and said we should not meet   *111*
again!

Father wept when he heard this and replied,

Fate is no friend of mine—
Such was my bitter thought.
But life has now become a happy thing indeed.

As I remembered my grief when Father had spoken of a "last
farewell" and afterwards those long years of waiting for his safe
return, I thought that I had never known such happiness. Father
said, "When I used to see men who had become old and decrepit
and yet insisted on pursuing their worldly activities, I regarded
their behaviour as the height of folly. I do not intend to follow
their example. From now on I shall stay here in retirement." It
made me very sad to realize that he no longer had any attachment
to the things and people of this world.   *112*

To the east the plain stretched out far in the distance, and we
had a clear view of the entire range of mountains from Hiei to   *113*
Inari. In the south one could clearly hear the sad sound of the
wind in the pine trees. "Rice fields" reached to the very side of   *114*
our house, and the bird-clappers gave the place a delightfully

rustic atmosphere. When the moon was bright, I used to stay up late at night enjoying the beauty of the scene. Since we lived so far away, people no longer came to visit me. One day, however, someone found an opportunity to send a message asking how I was. I replied,

> *No one person now remembers me and comes to call.*
> *But in the fences of this mountain place*
> 115 *The Autumn wind blows through the reeds.*

16 1039.x age 31

In the Tenth Month we moved back to the Capital. Mother had now become a nun and, though she stayed in the same house with Father and me, she lived separately from us. Father, who had more or less retired from the world, insisted that I should be mistress of the house. I felt most helpless and forlorn. One day a relation of ours, who had heard about my condition, sent a message suggesting that I should give up this idle, lonely life. In due 116 course I was invited to attend Court, but Father in his old-fashioned way thought that I would find life there very trying and he persuaded me to remain at home. Several people told him that he was mistaken. "Nowadays no young woman hesitates to serve at Court," said one of them. "All sorts of good things happen to people when they have taken service. Really, you should let her go and see what happens." So it was that Father reluctantly gave his consent.

My first period of service lasted exactly one night. When I went to the Palace, I wore a dark crimson robe of glossed silk over 117 eight thin under robes of dark red. Having been totally absorbed in Tales, I knew scarcely anyone except the people I used to visit in order to borrow books. Besides, I was so used to staying with my old-fashioned parents at home, gazing hour after hour at the

Bird-clappers gave the place
a delightfully rustic
atmosphere. (p. 81)

Autumn moon or the Spring blossoms, that when I arrived at Court I was in a sort of daze and hardly knew what I was doing. So at dawn on the following day I returned home.

During my cloistered years I had often imagined that life in the Palace would offer all sorts of pleasures which I never encountered in my monotonous routine at home. As it turned out, my first experience at Court suggested that I would feel extremely awkward and unhappy in these new surroundings. Yet *118* what could I do about it?

In the Twelfth Month I went to Court once more. I was given a room of my own, and this time I stayed in service for several days. When I was summoned to the Princess's apartments for night duty, I had to lie next to women I did not know and I could not sleep a wink. Overcome with nervousness and embarrassment, I wept secretly until dawn; then I returned to my room and spent all day in loving, anxious thoughts about Father, who was growing old and feeble and who depended on me so completely. I also thought of my poor nieces, who had lived with me ever since they lost their mother and who even used to sleep next to me, one on each side. As I sat in my room musing vacantly, I *119* had the impression that an eavesdropper was standing outside peeping on me, which made me most uncomfortable.

When I returned home after about ten days, Father and Mother had lit a fire in the hearth and were waiting for me. Seeing *120* me get out of the carriage, Father said, "When you were here, the house was full of visitors and attendants, but during the past days it has been completely silent and we have not seen a soul. It has been terribly sad and lonely. What will become of us if you stay at Court?" He burst into tears, and it was painful to see him in this state.

The next morning he said, "Now that you are back, the house is alive again. Look at all the people coming and going!"

The expression on his face as he sat there brought tears to my eyes. I wondered why my presence in the house should make such a difference. 121

They say that even for a Saint it is difficult to dream of a previous incarnation. Yet in my confused and aimless state I had the following dream in the chapel of Kiyomizu Temple. A man, evidently the Intendant, appeared before me and said, "In a previous incarnation you were a priest in this temple. As a carver of 122 many Buddhist images you accumulated great merit, and in your next incarnation you were born into a much better family than 123 before. It was you who carved the sixteen-foot statue of the Buddha in the eastern wing of this chapel. In fact you were covering it with gold foil when you died."

"Dear me!" I said. "In that case I had better gild it now."

"No. Someone else finished the job after your death. And it is he who dedicated the image."

If I had followed up this dream by a series of pious visits to Kiyomizu, things might have turned out well for me, since it was here that I had worshipped in that earlier incarnation. In my usual feckless way, however, I never bothered to make any further pilgrimages to the temple.

On the twenty-fifth day of the Twelfth Month I was summoned to the Princess's Court for the Naming of the Buddhas, 1039. xii. 25 124 and I went to stay in her palace for just one night. There were some forty ladies in attendance, all wearing dark red robes of glossed silk over white under robes. I tried to make myself inconspicuous by staying behind the lady who had first introduced me at Court, and in that great throng of people no one got a clear view of me.

I set out for home before daybreak the next morning when the snow was coming down in scattered flakes. In the freezing dawn the moon was dimly reflected on the glossy sleeves of my

I tried to make myself
inconspicuous. (p. 85)

dark red robe, and it seemed to me that the moon's face was wet with tears. These lines came to me, *125*

> *Sadly I see the year is drawing to an end*
> *And the night is giving way to dawn,*
> *While moonbeams wanly shine upon my sleeves.* *126*

If, having once entered service, I had continued in regular attendance, I should in due course have grown accustomed to this new life. Despite all my family distractions I could then have been accepted as a regular member of the Court instead of being regarded as an eccentric. But for reasons of their own my parents soon decided that I should stay at home.

Of course I had not expected that service at Court would suddenly lead to some brilliant improvement in my life; indeed there had been nothing very calculated about my decision to become a lady-in-waiting. The results fell even below my expectations, and in the end I composed this poem for myself,

> *How often have I picked the parsley by the river bank!*
> *And yet my wishes still are unfulfilled.* *127*

Things now became rather hectic for me. I forgot all about my *128* Tales and became much more conscientious. How could I have let all those years slip by, instead of practising my devotions and going on pilgrimages? I began to doubt whether any of my romantic fancies, even those that had seemed most plausible, had the slightest basis in fact. How could anyone as wonderful as Shining Genji or as beautiful as the girl whom Captain Kaoru kept hidden in Uji really exist in this world of ours? Oh, what a *129* fool I had been to believe such nonsense!

17 1042 age 34

Now that I was sincerely convinced of my errors and wanted to live a more serious life, I should have put my intentions into practice. This turned out to be impossible. I was told that no one at Court believed that I had actually retired to my home after my first period of service, and in the months that followed I was constantly being summoned to attend the Princess in her apartments. Since I was also ordered to bring my young nieces to Court, I was obliged to present them, and I myself had to make several appearances. But I had become far more modest in my desires and no longer had any great expectations.

Now that I was back in Court service—not through any wish of my own but because of my nieces—I could hardly be treated as a newcomer. On the other hand, I certainly did not qualify as one of those senior ladies-in-waiting who, from long experience at Court, go about with knowing looks on their faces and allow nothing to ruffle them. In consequence I was regarded rather scornfully as a sort of guest who came to Court for occasional visits. It was an awkward position. Yet, since I did not depend exclusively on my Court service, I was not particularly envious of the senior ladies; in fact I preferred my present situation, which allowed me to appear just when I was needed for service and to chat freely with other ladies-in-waiting when we were off duty. During ceremonies and other special occasions in the Palace I tried to keep to myself as much as possible; I liked to remain in the background and to get a general impression of what was happening rather than to become actively involved.

On a moonlit dawn in the Fourth Month I was part of the retinue that accompanied the Princess to the Imperial Palace. I decided to take advantage of this opportunity to go and worship my patron Goddess, Amaterasu, who was enshrined in this very building. That evening the moon shone brightly as I made my way in secret to the Sacred Mirror Room. Fortunately an old friend called Lady Hakase was able to act as my guide. By the

130

131

132

dim light of the hanging lantern she looked incredibly ancient and awe-inspiring. She spoke in the impressive voice one would expect from someone who had been in sacred service for so long, and I was convinced that she was no ordinary mortal but a manifestation of the Goddess Herself.

On the following evening the moon again was bright. I was sitting with some of the senior ladies-in-waiting by the open door of Fujitsubo Palace, gazing at the moon and conversing, when *133* we heard the elegant and impressive sound of Lady Umetsubo and her retinue proceeding to the Emperor's Palace. "If Her Majesty were still alive," said one of the ladies, "it would be she *134* who would now be on her way to the Emperor." I found this very moving and composed the poem,

> *Though now I dwell among the clouds,*
> *That Heavenly Door seems far away,*
> *And like the moon I fondly think upon the vanished past.* *135*

One night in Winter, when there was neither snow nor moon but the sky was clearly lit by the stars, I stayed up talking with the ladies in attendance on the Chancellor. We parted at *136* dawn and retired to our rooms. The next day the ladies sent me this poem in memory of our vigil,

> *Why should we think so fondly of a winter night*
> *When there was neither moon nor blossoms to be seen?*

Impressed that they should have shared my feelings about that night, I replied,

> *The ice which formed upon my sleeves*
> *On that chill wintry night*
> *Remains unmelted still,*
> *And the memory makes me shake all night with tears.* *137*

When I was sleeping near the Princess, I was awakened by a

sound from the garden. It was the water birds in the pond who were ceaselessly crying and flapping their wings. I murmured this poem,

> *Like me those water fowl who spend the night in restless sleep*
> *Now sadly shake the frost from off their wings.*

The lady-in-waiting who was lying beside me heard this and replied,

> *It is I who should be pitied,*
> *Who night after restless night*
> *Must doze here like those water birds*
> 138 *Who sadly brush the frost from off their wings.*

Once a lady-in-waiting with whom I was very friendly opened the sliding door between our two rooms, making them into a single large apartment, and we spent the day talking. A close friend of ours was in attendance on the Princess that day and *we?* sent several messages asking her to join us. Finally she replied that she would come if we had something "really important" to discuss. I sent the following poem attached to some withered reeds,

> 139 *Dry and withered like these winter reeds have we become*
> *While waiting for you here.*
> *No longer shall we crave your company*
> *But leave your coming to the wind.*

---

140 When distinguished visitors like High Court Nobles and Senior Courtiers came to the Palace, there were fixed rules about which ladies-in-waiting would receive them. An inexperienced outsider like me would certainly not be chosen; in fact I was so

18 1042
age 34

unimportant that such visitors would not even be aware of my existence. On a very dark night in the early part of the Tenth Month, while some priests were chanting the Perpetual Sacred Readings in the most beautiful voices, I and another lady-in-waiting stayed near the door of the chapel. As we lay there, chatting and listening to the priests, a gentleman approached. "We could run and fetch one of the ladies from the inner apartments," said my companion, "but it would make a bad impression. Never mind! We must adapt ourselves to circumstances. Let's just stay and see how things turn out!" While she got up and spoke to the gentleman, I lay where I was and listened to their conversation. He talked in a quiet, gentle way and I could tell that he was a man of perfect qualities. "And who may your companion be?" I heard him say; but there was none of the crude, lecherous tone in his voice that one would expect from most men who asked this sort of question. Then he started speaking about the sadness of the world and other such matters, and there was something so sensitive about his manner that, for all my usual shyness, I found it hard to remain stiff and aloof. I therefore joined my companion and the gentleman. "So there is still a young lady in this Palace whom I do not know!" he said, surprised to hear my voice, and he gave no sign of wanting to leave.

It was a dark, starless night and the rain made a delightful patter on the leaves. "There is a special elegance and charm" he said "about dark nights like this. Do you ladies not agree? If everything were lit up by the moon, the brightness would only embarrass one."

He spoke about the different beauties of Spring and Autumn. "Each has its own delight," he said. "On Spring nights the sky is beautifully shrouded with mist. The moon then is not too bright and its light seems to be floating away in the distance. How delightful it is at such a time to hear someone plucking gently at the strings of a lute that have been set in the key of the Fragrant

141

142

143

144

145

146 Breeze! When Autumn comes the sky is still misty, but the lucent moon shines through so clearly that one feels one could pick it up in one's hands. The soughing of the wind and the hum of the insects blend in such a way that all the savours of Nature seem to have come together. At such moments the strumming of the great zither accompanied by the clear notes of a flute makes one wonder how one could ever have admired Spring. But then there is a Winter night when the sky is chill, the air bitter cold, and the piles of snow reflect the moonlight. Then the tremulous sound of the flageolet makes one forget about both Spring and Autumn." So he continued for a while, before asking us which season we liked best. My companion named Autumn as her favourite, but I decided to answer with a poem,

> The hazy Springtime moon—
> That is the one I love,
> When light green sky and fragrant blooms
147 Are all alike enwrapped in mist.

He repeated my lines several times. "So you turn down the Autumn nights!" he said and added his own poem,

> Should I be spared to live beyond tonight,
> Spring evenings will remain within my heart
148 In memory of how we met.

My companion, who had declared her preference for Autumn, composed the verse,

> It seems your hearts have all been drawn to Spring.
149 Am I alone to gaze at Autumn moons?

The gentleman seemed greatly interested in our conversation.

"Even in China" he said "people have always found it hard to choose between Spring and Autumn. Surely there must be

some special reason that you ladies have made up your minds so
clearly. At times when I am deeply moved by something, whether
it be sad or happy, the particular aspect of nature at that moment,
the look of the sky or the moon or the blossoms, sinks deeply into
my heart. I wonder what made you two decide as you did about
your seasons. Since ancient times the moon on Winter nights has
been considered a depressing thing. Most people have found it   *150*
too cold to be worth admiring, but I recall that my own feelings
on one such night were very different.

"I had gone to Ise as an Imperial Envoy to attend the coming-of-age ceremony of the High Priestess. Intending to return to   *151*
the Capital at dawn, I got up very early and saw the moonlight
brightly reflected in the snow, which had been piling up for days.
So it would be under such a sky that I should have to make my
journey, I thought gloomily as I went to take leave of Her Holi-
ness. Her apartment was unlike anything I had ever seen, and I
was overcome with awe at the thought that this was where the
High Priestess actually lived. She summoned me to one of her
rooms, which was splendidly arranged in a manner befitting the
occasion. Among the attendants were people who had been in
Ise ever since the reign of Emperor Enyū. There was something   *152*
remarkably impressive and elegant about their old-fashioned
appearance as they sat there tearfully recounting stories from the
ancient past. Then a beautifully tuned lute was brought out and
one of the attendants played for us. It all seemed to belong to
another world.

"As dawn approached I regretted having to return to the
Capital and decided not to set out until later. Ever since, snowy
winter nights have moved me deeply. Though I may be huddled
by a brazier, I will leave it in the bitterest cold to go out on the
veranda and gaze at the snow. No doubt you ladies also have
some personal reason for feeling as you do about your seasons. In

Then a beautifully tuned lute
was brought out. (p. 93)

the future I too shall probably be deeply moved by dark rainy nights like this. I confess that they now seem just as charming as that snowy night in the apartment of the High Priestess."

After he had finished speaking and had left us, it occurred to me that he still had no idea who I was.

In the Eight Month of the following year I again accompanied the Princess to the Imperial Palace. There was a concert that lasted all night in the Senior Courtiers' Chamber. Among those present was the gentleman I had met on that rainy night; but, having no idea that he was there, I stayed in my room.

Late at night I pushed open the sliding door and looked out. A faint moon hovered in the dawning sky. As I gazed at the beautiful scene outside, I heard footsteps approaching the veranda and then the voice of a man chanting a sutra. He stopped directly in front of my room and said something. As he heard my reply, it all seemed to come back to him. "I have never forgotten that rainy night," he said, "not even for a moment. How I long back to it!" Since there was no time for a proper answer, I said these lines,

> *How could it stay so clearly in your mind?*
> *There was nothing but the patter of the rain on leaves.*

Hardly had I finished when his companions joined him, so I slipped quietly into the back of my room without waiting for his answer.

Since I left the Imperial Palace before morning, he called on the companion who had been with me at our first meeting, and it was from her that I got his reply, "If we should ever have another such rainy night, I should like to play the flute for you. I shall play my very best." I wanted to hear him and waited for a suitable time. It never came.

One quiet Spring evening I heard that he was visiting the Princess's Palace. I was about to creep out of my room with my companion, but there were many people outside by the veranda

1043. viii
Age 35

1044. Spring
Age 36

and the reception rooms were crowded with the usual throng. So I gave up and retired to my room. He must have had the same feelings as I. It appeared that he had specially visited the Palace in the hope of a quiet evening, then because of all the hubbub had left without even seeing me. I simply wrote this poem, and that was the end of it all,

Did you know what burnt within my breast,
Oh fisherman by the Bay of Naruto,
As I waited till I was alone
To row my boat to Kashima?

He was an unusual man with a serious character, not the type to bustle about asking what had become of me or of my companion.

19

Now I really began to regret having wasted so much time on my silly fancies, and I bitterly reproached myself for not having accompanied Mother and Father on their pilgrimages. My position had greatly improved, both in social standing and in material wealth, and I had also succeeded in rearing my little bud exactly as I wished. The time had come, I told myself, to think about preparing for my life in the world to come. Towards the end of the Eleventh Month I set out on a pilgrimage to Ishiyama. The country was beautiful under the heavy snow. When I reached Ōsaka Barrier, I remembered that the last time I had come this way it had also been Winter and that there had been a fierce wind. I wrote the poem,

There is no difference in their sounds—
This wind that blows across the Barrier now
And the one I heard so many years ago.

160 Gazing at the magnificent structure of Seki Temple, I recalled that on my journey to the Capital I had seen only the roughly hewn statue of the Buddha, and I was greatly moved to think how 161 much time had passed. Uchiide Beach had not changed in the slightest since I last saw it.

162 Reaching Ishiyama at sunset, we first went to the bath house and, after purifying ourselves, proceeded to the temple. There was not a voice to be heard; the only sound was the fearful howling of the mountain wind. I dozed off without finishing my prayers, and presently someone said to me, "Sacred incense has been bestowed upon us from the main temple. Go there quickly and tell them!" At that I woke up and realized it had been a dream. Thinking it might be an auspicious omen, I spent the rest of the night in prayer.

The next day it was still snowing and there was a terrible gale. I felt very downhearted and tried to comfort myself by talking to a woman with whom I had become friendly at Court and who had accompanied me on this pilgrimage. We left the temple after a retreat of three days.

20 1046. X
age 38

163 In the Tenth Month of the following year I heard that the Sacred Purification for the Great Festival of Thanksgiving was to take place on the twenty-fifth day. Despite all the excitement I began to observe abstinence in preparation for a pilgrimage to 164 Hase Temple and arranged to leave for Hase on the very day of the Purification ceremony. My brother was outraged. "This is a ceremony that you can witness only once in an Imperial reign," he said. "People are coming all the way from the country to see it. When there are so many days in the year, it is madness to choose precisely this one to leave the Capital. You'll be a laughingstock

for generations to come." My husband, however, told me I should do exactly as I wished, and I was impressed by his understanding.

The people who were to accompany me on my pilgrimage all wanted to see the ceremony in the Capital and I was sorry for them. But what benefit does one gain from these ceremonies? Surely Buddha would look with particular favour on people who chose such a time for a pilgrimage, and this would earn them special merit.

Having firmly made up my mind, I set out from the Capital at dawn with my attendants all dressed in pure white robes. As we went along the Second Avenue, where the Imperial Procession was to pass, I ordered my forerunners to carry sacred tapers. The crowds, who were hurrying pell-mell towards the galleries, some on horseback, others in carriages, others on foot, were amazed to see our group. "Who on earth can they be?" people said, laughing uneasily, and some of them actually jeered at us.

When we passed the house of Yoshiyori, the Captain of the Middle Palace Guards, the gates were wide open and His Excellency was evidently about to set off for the galleries. The attendants who were standing by the gates laughed at us. "Off on a pilgrimage, are they? What a day to choose!" There was one man among them who seemed to have more sense. "What good does it really do us to see the Purification?" he asked in a serious tone. "Those devout folk setting off on their pilgrimage are sure to receive Buddha's favour. It's we who are the stupid ones. We'd have done far better to go on a pilgrimage ourselves rather than spend the day in sightseeing."

Having started early in order to get past the crowds before daylight, we stopped at the Great Gate of Hōsō Temple to let the latecomers catch up with us and also to wait for a clearing in the mist, which was still terrifyingly thick. Now we had a proper view of the sightseers flowing in from the country like a great river. The road was so blocked that the people could hardly get by.

I set out from the Capital at dawn. (p. 101)

As our carriage started off again and we tried to make our way through the shoals of people, I noticed the look of amazement on their faces. Even ignorant-looking, shabby little children were taken aback when they saw us. Though I had set out on my pilgrimage with the most serious determination, I began to have doubts at the sight of all these people. However, I prayed devoutly to Buddha and finally reached the ferry at Uji.   *170*

Here too there were great crowds. Seeing how many passengers wanted to cross, the boatmen had assumed a haughty air; they stood with their sleeves tucked up, leaning against the poles by the river, smugly humming and whistling their boat songs, and refusing to hurry up with the ferry. We waited for ages but   *171* nothing happened, and so I had a good look at the surroundings. It was here, I remembered, that the princesses in Lady Murasaki's Tale had lived. When reading the book, I had wondered why Captain Kaoru should have chosen this particular place to install his mistress; now I saw what a beautiful spot it was. I was still lost in reverie when the ferry finally arrived and we were able to cross. On reaching the opposite shore, I went to visit the Chancellor's villa, where my first thought was that Lady Ukifune must   *172* have lived in just such a building.

Since we had left the Capital before daybreak, my servants were exhausted and we stopped to rest at a place called Yahirouchi. We were just having something to eat when to my horror I heard one of the men say, "Surely that's the famous Mount   *173* Kurikoma. It's getting dark. We'd better put all our things to-   *174* gether and get started."

We crossed the mountain safely and reached Nieno Pond just as the sun was setting over the hills. The men went off in different directions to look for some place to spend the night. "It's hard to find anywhere suitable in these parts," said one of them   *175* when he returned. "All I've seen is a simple peasants' cottage."

"Well, it can't be helped," I said. "We'll have to stay there."

There was no one in the cottage except two rough fellows who explained that their masters had gone to the Capital. These men did not sleep a wink all night, but kept walking about inside and outside the house. "What are you men doing?" asked one of my women. The men, who obviously thought that I was asleep and would not hear them, replied, "Good heavens! We can't possibly go to sleep. Here we are putting up people we know nothing about. What would happen to us if they made off with the cauldron? That's why we're walking about like this." I found it all rather weird but could not help being amused.

We left early the next morning and stopped to pray at Tōdai Temple. Isonokami Shrine was quite as old as its name implied and had fallen into ruins. That night we stayed in a temple in a place called Yamanobē. I was utterly exhausted but managed to recite my sutras before dozing off. I dreamt that I had come to a place where the wind was blowing fiercely and where I saw a very beautiful and impressive-looking woman. When she caught sight of me, she asked with a smile, "Why have you come here?"

"How could I possibly not have come?" I replied. "You are hoping to become a lady-in-waiting in the Imperial Palace," she said. "For this purpose you must look to Lady Hakase for help." When I woke up, I felt happy and encouraged, and prayed more fervently than ever to Buddha.

We crossed Hase River the next day and reached the temple by nightfall. After performing my ablutions, I went up to the temple, where I spent three days in retreat. On the eve of my return to the Capital I thought that I saw a person from the Main Hall who put something before me with the words, "Look! This is a branch of *sugi* bestowed on you from Inari as a token of special favour." When I woke up, I realized it had been a dream.

We left Hase Temple before dawn. On our way back to the Capital we could not find any proper lodging for the night and were obliged to stay on the far side of Nara Slope in another

After performing my
ablutions, I went up to the
temple. (p. 104)

simple little cottage. "There's something strange about this place," one of my people warned me. "Don't fall asleep whatever you do! If anything unusual happens, just stay quiet and pretend you have heard nothing! Try to breathe as softly as possible!" I was terrified, and the night seemed longer than a thousand years. When dawn finally came, I was told that the place was a thieves' den and that the mistress of the house had been up to something suspicious during the night.

It was a very windy day when we returned on the Uji ferry. We passed near the weirs and I wrote this poem,

These Uji weirs that I have only heard described—
I pass them now so closely in our boat
That I can even see the waves that ripple on the stakes.

Anyone reading this account of visits to one temple after another might well imagine that I was forever going on pilgrimages. In fact there were long intervals, often several years, between my retreats.

In Spring I made a pilgrimage to Kurama. The mountainside was beautifully veiled in mist. Some people brought us yam roots from the hills, which delighted me. On our return from the temple the blossoms had all scattered and the countryside had lost its charm; but in the Tenth Month when I went there on a further retreat the scenery was lovelier than ever. The mountainside was a great cloth of brocade, and in the streams the water bubbled like drops of crystal. When I reached the presbytery, I was overcome by the beauty of the maple leaves, which had been besprinkled by an Autumn shower, and I composed this poem,

21 1047
age 39

Some people brought us
yam roots. (p. 107)

What rain has sprinkled on these leaves
That they glow an even brighter red
Than the mountain's rich brocade?   183

I returned to Ishiyama a couple of years after my previous pilgrimage. It seemed to be raining heavily all night long. What
a nuisance rain was for travellers, I thought as I opened the lattice
and looked out. By the light of the pale moon I could see all the
way to the bottom of the valley. Then I realized that what had
sounded like rain was water flowing at the base of the trees,

> *I thought it was the rain,*
> *That valley stream which flows between the trees.*
> *But the moon shines clearly in the dawning sky,*
> *More beautiful than any I have seen.*   184

When I again set out on a retreat to Hase, I was far more
hopeful of success than on my first visit. The journey took longer
than usual, since many people had provided hospitality on the
way. In Hahaso Wood in Yamashiro the Autumn foliage was at
its height. Crossing Hase River, I composed this verse, which
surely augured well for my pilgrimage,

> *Like the waves that lap against the river banks*
> *I too have returned.*
> *This time I shall most certainly receive*
> *The sugi's full effect.*   185

We returned to the Capital after three days in the temple,
but this time there were too many people in our party for us to
stay in the little house by Nara Slope. My men built a temporary
hut for me in the field and I slept there while they bedded down

22

1047

109

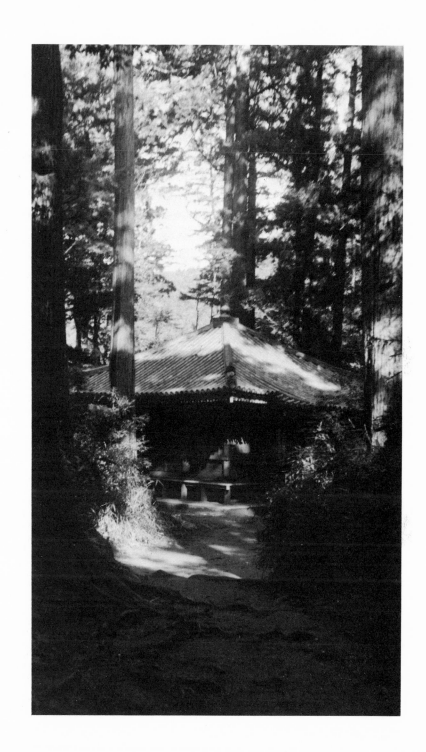

under the open sky, lying on their leather leg-pieces, which they had spread on the grass and covered with straw matting. In the morning their hair was damp with dew. The moon was wonderfully clear and beautiful that dawn, and I wrote the poem,

> *Even as I wander on my journey*
> *It always stays above me in the sky—*
> *This moon at dawn,*
> *This moon I gazed on in the Capital.*

Now that I was able to do exactly as I wished, I went on one distant pilgrimage after another. Some were delightful, some difficult, but I found great solace in them all being confident that they would bring me future benefit. No longer having any sorrows of my own, I concentrated on providing the best possible upbringing for my children and waited impatiently for them to grow up. I also prayed for my husband's future, and I was confident that my prayers would be answered.

23

1048
age 40

There was a woman who had once been an intimate friend, and we were always sending each other poems. With the passing of time our relations had naturally become less close, but we still kept up an active correspondence. Then she married the Governor of Echizen and accompanied him to his province, after which I heard no more from her. I managed to send this poem,

> *Even the constant flame of friendship*
> *That burnt so long between us two*
> *Has now been buried in the deep north snows.*

She replied:

Even the little stones remain,
Though buried by Mount Shira's snow.
So how can our bright flame be quenched?

In the beginning of the Third Month I went to a secluded part
of the Western Hills where not a soul was to be seen and where
everything was peacefully shrouded in mist. There was nothing
but the mass of flowers that blossomed desolately on the hillside,
and I wrote this poem,

1049 **24**
age 41

Here they grow in mountain depths
Far from any dwelling place,
And no one comes to view their blooms.

190

At a time when my marriage was going badly, I set out for   191
Uzumasa on a retreat and, while I was there, received a message
from a woman with whom I had become friendly during my stay
in the Palace. I was composing my reply when I heard the booming of the temple bell, and so I added the poem,

1049 **25**
age 41

Even here I cannot shun
The clamour of this sad world.
For the tolling of the vesper bell
Forlornly stirs my heart.

26

Once when I was serving in the beautiful and serene Palace of the little Princess I spent the entire day chatting with a couple of close friends. After I returned home on the following day, I found myself missing them badly, so to while away the time, I composed this poem,

> *She who dives into the waves*
> *Is bound to wet her sleeves.*
> *Yet fondly I recall our days*
> *As fellow divers by the sea.*

192

One of my companions replied,

> *Together we scoured the windswept coast,*
> *But found no shells that we could use,*
> *And only our sleeves were spattered by the surf.*

And the other:

> *Had she not hoped to find some seaweed growing in the bay,*
> *This diver never would have searched the windswept shore,*
> *Peering for some gap among the waves.*

27 *1050 age 42*

193 There was another person with whom I had been on close terms. We used to discuss the gloomy and delightful and bitter things of this world. Then she went down to Chikuzen. One bright moonlit night after she had left, I lay thinking fondly about a similar evening when I had met this friend in the Princess's Palace and stayed up with her, gazing at the moon and not getting a wink of sleep all night. I dozed off and dreamt that we had met in the same palace and talked to each other just as we used to do in reality. When I awoke, the moon hung near the western ridge of the hills. Realizing that it had been a dream, I lay there sunk

in deep reflection and wished I had never woken up. I composed 194
this poem,

I saw her in my dream,
And now my bed is all afloat with tears.
Tell her how much I yearn for her,
Oh moon, as now you glide towards the West!

In the Autumn I had occasion to go down to Izumi. After
Yodo the country became more beautiful and impressive than I 195
can say. We spent the night on our boat in Takahama. Late at
night, when it was extremely dark, I detected the sound of oars.
Someone asked who was there and I was told that it was a woman
singer. My people became very interested and called for her boat
to be rowed alongside ours. By the distant light of the flares I
could see the woman standing there in an unlined dress with long
sleeves, hiding her face with a fan as she sang for us. It was a very
moving sight.

On the following evening we reached the Bay of Sumiyoshi
just as the sun was sinking over the mountain top. I have never
seen a painting to equal the beauty of this scene—the pine branches
and the sky all shrouded by mist, the surface of the sea, the waves
breaking on the beach,

How shall I describe it,
To what shall I compare it—
This Bay of Sumiyoshi on an Autumn eve?

I gazed about me as we rowed along, after we had passed, I
kept looking back and felt that I could never have enough.

It was Winter when we returned to the Capital, embarking
at the Bay of Ōtsu. On our first night the rain came down vio-

We reached the Bay of
Sumiyoshi. (p. 115)

lently, and the gale was fierce enough to dislodge the very rocks. The roar of the waves as they beat against the shore and the wild howling of the wind put me in such a state of terror that I thought my last day had come. The men pulled our boat onto the dunes, and there we spent the night.

Eventually the rain stopped, but the gale still made it impossible to launch the boat and we had to waste several days on the beach. When finally the wind began to die down, I raised the blinds in my cabin and looked out. The evening tide was swiftly rising, and I was charmed by the loud cry of the cranes that had come into the bay. A company of men arrived from the Provincial Office and informed us that, if we had left Ōtsu on our first evening and tried to make for Ishizu, our boat would surely have capsized and disappeared without a trace. I listened to them gloomily and wrote the lines, *196*

If we had embarked on that rough sea before the storm blew up,
And vanished in the waves of Ishizu . . . *197*

What with one thing and another my life had been full of worries. My career at Court might have turned out well if only I had settled down to my duties from the outset and persevered; but, since my attendance was always being interrupted, I never had a chance to get ahead. Now it was too late. I was past my prime and realized that the time had come to abandon my youthful hopes. Besides I was rapidly losing my health and could no longer go on pilgrimages as I wished; soon I had to give up even the occasional retreat. I did not feel that I would live very long and was determined to do everything possible for my children *198*

29

1057-58
age 49

during the years that remained. Their future was a constant source of concern.

My husband was due for an appointment and we waited for it anxiously. The announcement finally came in the Autumn, but it was not nearly as good as we had hoped and we were bitterly disappointed. I was told that his new province was nearer the Capital than the eastern districts that I knew so well from Father's time. So I resigned myself to the inevitable and made hasty preparations for my husband's departure. It was decided that he would leave the Capital about the tenth day of the Eighth Month, setting out from the house into which his daughter had recently moved. We had no way of knowing how things would turn out, and the last days were very lively, with lots of people gathered round us in high spirits.

When he left on the twenty-seventh, he was accompanied by our boy. The lad, dressed in a scarlet under robe of glossy silk, a hunting cloak of light purple with a green lining, and figured silk trousers also of light purple, set off carrying his sword. In front of him went his father, who wore bluish grey trousers of figured silk and a hunting cloak. They mounted their horses beside the covered gallery.

After all the commotion of their departure, I found time hanging heavily on my hands. Yet I did not feel quite as unhappy as I had been when I first heard about the appointment, for now I knew that his province was not too far away. On the following day the people who had accompanied my husband's procession on the first leg of his journey came back and reported that he had made a brilliant departure. One of them added, "This morning a huge human fire sprang up near the procession and moved towards the Capital." I took this to mean that the fire was for one of the men accompanying my husband. How could I have guessed what the omen really meant?

During the months that followed I devoted myself to taking

care of my children, and in the Fourth Month of the following year my husband returned to the Capital to spend the Summer and the Autumn at home.

On the twenty-fifth day of the Ninth Month he was taken ill, and on the fifth of the Tenth Month he faded away like a dream. Never have I known such sorrow. I remembered that, when Mother had dedicated a mirror at Hase Temple, the priest had dreamt about a weeping figure rolling on the floor. Such was my present state. There had been no happy person in the priest's dream; nor could I expect any happiness in my own life.

We cremated him on the evening of the twenty-third and he vanished with the smoke. My boy, whom I had seen off the previous Autumn when he had accompanied his father from the Capital, brilliantly attired and much praised by everyone, now wore a sad white tunic over his black robes. As I watched him walking along in tears beside the hearse, inexpressible thoughts flooded through me; it was as though I had moved straight into a dream. I felt that my husband was looking down at me in my wretchedness.

If only I had not given myself over to Tales and poems since my young days but had spent my time in religious devotions, I should have been spared this misery. After my first pilgrimage to Hase, when I had dreamt that someone threw an object before me and said that it was a branch of *sugi* bestowed from Inari as a special token, I should have gone directly on a pilgrimage to the Inari Shrines. Then things would not have turned out like this. The interpreter had explained that all those dreams about praying to the Heavenly Goddess meant that I would become an Imperial nurse, serve in the Imperial Palace, and receive the special favour of Their Majesties; but none of this had come true. Alas, the only thing that had turned out exactly as predicted was the sad image in the mirror. So I had wandered through life without realizing any of my hopes or accumulating any merit.

1058.ix. ~ x.

204
205
206
207
208
209
210
211

Amida Buddha was standing
in the far end of our garden.
(p. 121)

Yet we continue to live despite all our suffering. I was greatly
worried that my expectations for the future world would also be
disappointed, and my only hope was the dream I remembered
from the thirteenth night of the Tenth Month of the third year
of Tenki. Then I had dreamt that Amida Buddha was standing   212
in the far end of our garden. I could not see Him clearly, for a
layer of mist seemed to separate us, but when I peered through
the mist I saw that He was about six foot tall and that the lotus
pedestal on which He stood was about four foot off the ground.
He glowed with a golden light, and one of His hands was
stretched out, while the other formed a magical sign. He was in-   213
visible to everyone but me. I had been greatly impressed but at
the same time frightened and did not dare move near my blinds
to get a clearer view of Him. He had said, "I shall leave now, but
later I shall return to fetch you." And it was only I who could
hear His voice. Thereafter it was on this dream alone that I set
my hopes for salvation.

30
(1055)

Until now I had lived in the same house as my nephews, but   214
after these sad events we separated and I rarely had a chance to see
them. One dark night, however, my nephew who had moved to
Rokuhara came to visit me. It was strange to see him again, and I   215
gave him this poem,

Why have you come this moonless night
*To visit one who dwells in Obasute's dark recess?**   216

31

*Obasute means "abandoned aunt."

121

32

To a close friend from whom I had heard nothing since my husband's death I sent the poem,

Do you suppose that I have left this world?
Alas, I linger on in tears.

33

? 1059

In the Tenth Month there was a very bright moon. Weeping, I gazed at it and wrote,

How bright the moonlight shines,
Although my eyes are ever fogged with tears!

34

Many years have passed, but whenever I think about that sad, dreamlike time my heart is thrown into turmoil and my eyes darken, so that even now I cannot clearly remember all that happened.

My family went to live elsewhere, and I stayed forlornly by myself in the old house. One day when I was thinking bitterly of my sad condition I sent this poem to someone from whom I had not heard for a long time,

Wildly the sagebrush grows
Outside this house where no one comes to call,
And my tears well up
Like the drops of dew upon those leaves.

217

It was a nun to whom I sent my poem, and she replied,

Your sagebrush and your dew belong to worldly homes.
Think how overgrown the thickets are
In the cell of one who finally renounced the world!

Abbreviations used in notes

Notes

NKB: Nihon Koten Bungaku Taikei edition of *Genji Monogatari* (Tokyo, 1964).

PBk: Ivan Morris, *The Pillow Book of Sei Shōnagon*, Volume 2 (London: Oxford University Press; New York: Columbia University Press, 1967).

SNHyo: Kazuichirō Miyata, *Sarashina Nikki Hyōshaku* (Kyoto, 1931).

WSP: Ivan Morris, *The World of the Shining Prince* (London: Oxford University Press; New York, Alfred A. Knopf, Inc., 1964).

1.   The first sentence of the book is the only one to be written specifically in the third person: Literally, "How rustic must a/the person be who grew up. . . !" Obviously this refers to the author herself, who grew up in the province of Kazusa (map 1), where her father had become Assistant Governor in 1017 at the age of forty. The end of the Great East Road is the province of Hitachi. The journey from Heian Kyō (the Capital) to Kazusa was longer than to Hitachi, though the actual distance was shorter. There is also a reference to a poem by Ki no Tomonori (late ninth century).

> *Oh, how I long to join you!*
> *The Sash Festival of Hitachi,*
> *At the end of the Great East Road,*
> *Will bring me to your side.*

(I.e., the festival will be my pretext for going to see you in Hitachi.) For the contemporary attitude toward the provinces (scorn, fear, depression) see WSP, pp. 95–96. The journey from Kazusa to the Capital took Lady Sarashina and her family exactly three months; by present-day express train it takes four hours. In terms of the time required for travel Japan was about five hundred times larger for her than for a Japanese person today.

2.   Tales (*monogatari*): in its broadest sense the term refers to Japanese narrative prose in general, but it is usually limited to prose fiction written between the ninth and sixteenth centuries. The earliest extant

123

monogatari belong to the tenth century. The genre developed remarkably during the course of the century and culminated in *The Tale of Genji*. "Tale" is not a very satisfactory translation of *monogatari*, but it is less misleading than "novel" or "romance." *The Tale of Genji* was a psychological novel, the first in the history of world literature, but none of the other *monogatari* that have come down to us can be so described.

3. The Shining Prince refers to Prince Genji, the principal hero of Murasaki Shikibu's great novel. "It is said that the name Shining Prince was given to him by the Korean [visitors to the Capital] who admired him so greatly." (NKB, I, 151.)

4. Bhêchadjaguru (Yakushi Hotoke), the Buddha of Healing. This popular Buddha was worshipped mainly to obtain health and longevity, but people came to Him with other wishes also. It was customary at the time to get religious images built in one's own height. This was supposed to increase their efficacy.

5. This was a temporary, intermediate residence chosen to avoid an unlucky direction or to obtain release from a future taboo (for details see PBk, note 103). People setting off on a journey carefully chose an auspicious day; when the day came, they left their old house and moved into a nearby temporary house before actually starting on their journey. In the present case Takasue (Lady Sarashina's father) and his party spent about a fortnight in the temporary house at Imatachi before leaving for the Capital. Daily life in Heian times, which was inconvenient enough at the best of times, was full of such gratuitous complications.

6. They crossed the border between Kazusa and Shimōsa, and stayed in Ikata (or Iketa) near the present-day city of Chiba (map 1). The original text has Shimotsuke for Shimōsa; this was either Lady Sarashina's mistake (see Introduction, pp. 17–18) or that of a later copyist.

7. Mano no Chō. *Manoshitera* in the original text is certainly a mistake.

8. The poems in Lady Sarashina's book are all thirty-one syllable *tanka* constructed in 5 lines of 5–7–5–7–7 syllables. See Introduction, pp. 25–26.

9. Kagami Rapids on Futoi River: the lower reaches of present-day Edo River in Chiba Prefecture near Tokyo; probably Matsusato corresponds to present-day Matsudo City (map 1).

10. Because, according to Shinto beliefs, the nurse was ritually defiled by childbirth and her presence might have endangered the travellers on their journey.

11. People in the Heian period, even members of the aristocracy, usually slept in and under their clothes; there does not appear to have been anything designed especially as bed clothing.

12. A prophetic observation: Musashi is the site of present-day Tokyo. *Murasaki*: a perennial plant, something like gromwell, about two feet long, with white flowers and deep purple roots, used for making purple dye. The dictionary gives *Lithospermum erythrorhizon; murasaki* has a more attractive sound, and I have retained it in my translation. *Murasaki* plants had a famous poetic association with the Plain of Musashi:

> *Because of the single* murasaki *plant*
> *The grasses in Musashi Plain*
> *Have all become so beautiful.*

13. Takeshiba: probably on the site of the present-day Seikai Temple in Minato Ward, Tokyo.

14. Haha Estate: this was the name of a *shōen*, one of the multifarious estates held by members of the aristocracy or by religious institutions, whose objective was to secure certain privileges for their land, notably tax exemption. The *shōen* became the characteristic economic unit in the Heian period. The aristocracy lived largely on income from the *shōen*, though of course they are hardly ever mentioned in the literature of the time.

15. Family name: *saka* in the original text is probably a mistake for *sō* (*sau, kabane*—family name); according to another theory, however, it is a mistake for *sō* (*sau, shō*—manor house). Miyata interprets *saka* to mean "slope," but there is no evidence of any place called Takeshiba Slope.

16. Fire huts (*hitakiya*): small, roofless huts built in the Palace gardens to house the bonfires that provided illumination, especially during nocturnal festivals and ceremonies.

17. . . . can see none of it: I follow the commentators who give *mide* for *mite*. *Mite* seems to make no sense at all.

18. The Princess implies that she is impelled by a karma from a previous incarnation, and the man from Musashi is aware of this motivation.

19. Bridge of Seta: famous bridge across Seta River in Ōmi Province at the southern tip of Lake Biwa (map 2); it figures frequently in classical literature. Span (*ma*), which I have translated as "section," was the standard measure for rooms, halls, etc. A *ma* was the distance between two adjacent pillars in a Heian mansion, being about 3.3 yards in length.

20. A creature of great fragrance: i.e., the Princess, who was no doubt heavily scented. Of course the people who saw the guard could not possibly have guessed what he was carrying.

21. Leave my traces in this province (*ato wo taru*): the Princess refers to the current doctrine of *honji suijaku* (*ato taru* being the Japanese reading of the Sino-Japanese *suijaku*), according to which the Shinto gods were manifestations of the Buddhas. *Honji* was the "true place" (i.e., the essence or noumenon) of the Buddhas and Bodhisattvas; *suijaku* were the "traces" or "tracks" that they left when assuming the forms of Shinto gods, holy men, etc., as they passed through the world of phenomena. The doctrine of *honji suijaku* appears to have referred originally to the two parts of the Lotus Sutra, but by the time of Lady Sarashina it had become an underlying theory of Buddhist-Shinto syncretism. Just as the true Buddhas "left their traces" in the Shinto gods of Japan, so the Princess was fated to "leave her traces" in the remote wilds of Musashi Province.

22. Because, among other things, she had been polluted by sexual intercourse with a man of a lower class and could not possibly resume her Imperial position.

23. The man was of far too humble birth to be appointed Governor of a province or to be made legal guardian or lord of its Imperial estates.

24. Asudagawa in the original is almost certainly an error for Sumida-gawa, in which case Sagami is an error for Shimōsa. This paragraph refers to the following passage from Section 9 of *Ise Monogatari* ("The Tales of Ise"), a ninth-century collection of stories centered on Japanese poems, traditionally attributed to Ariwara no Narihira and largely concerned with his romantic exploits and poetic reactions. This is the passage:

They continued on their way and came to the large river between the provinces of Musashi and Shimōsa, which is called Sumida River. Standing in a group by the bank of the river, they were all sunk in thought, remembering the great distance they had journeyed from the Capital. But the ferryman interrupted them with a cry of "Come aboard! It's getting dark." When they were aboard and about to cross the great river, they were overcome by sorrow; for each of them had left behind someone he loved. Just then they caught sight of a white bird, about the size of a snipe, with red beak and legs, who was skimming over the water looking for fish. None of them had seen such a bird in the Capital and they asked the ferryman about it. "We call it the Capital Bird," he said. Hearing this, [the hero] produced the following poem:

> *If to that name you be but true,*
> *Oh, Bird of the Capital,*
> *Tell me one thing:*
> *Is she I love alive or dead?*

At this everyone in the group burst into tears.

Miyakadori (Capital Bird) refers either to an oyster catcher or a black-headed gull (*larus ridibundus*).

25. Narihira: here he is identified as Ari Go Chūjō, which means "the Middle Captain of the Inner Palace Guards, the fifth son of the Ariwara family." Ariwara no Narihira (825–880): famous poet, known for his good looks and amorous exploits; classed as one of the Six Poetical Geniuses; reputed hero and author of "The Tales of Ise" or part of it (see note 24).

26. Nishitomi: near the modern city of Fujisawa (map 1).

27. Morokoshi Plain: near either Fujisawa or Ōiso on Sagami Nada. The *nadeshiko* (*dianthus superbus*, fringed pink, Japanese pink or carnation)

is regarded as a peculiarly Japanese flower. Lady Sarashina uses the word *Yamato-nadeshiko* ("Japanese *nadeshiko*"), which later came to mean "the flower of Japanese womanhood."

28. Mount Ashigara: presentday Mount Hakone, a popular mountain resort that can be reached from Tokyo in a couple of hours. *Hi* ("days") in the text is usually taken to be a mistake for *ri* ("mile").

29. *Asobi* was a general term for female entertainers who sang, played music, danced, etc., and who also served as prostitutes. "Singer" is probably the best translation but it is only approximate.

30. Naniwa corresponds in general to modern Osaka. The singers imply that they were as skilful as those from Naniwa. Until at least the eighteenth century the general level of artistic accomplishment was always higher in the west of Japan, i.e., near the Capital, than in the eastern provinces including Edo (Tokyo).

31. *Aoi: asarum caulescens*, a form of snake-weed or bistort with paired, flesh-colored blossoms. They were associated with the great Aoi Matsuri (Festival) in the Fourth Month and therefore reminiscent of the Capital, where such festivals were held.

32. Refers to Yokobashiri Barrier on the border of Sagami and Suruga Provinces. Barriers were erected on all provincial borders and also in strategic mountain passes like Hakone, which protected the western region of Japan from the relatively untamed East. Travellers were inspected and sometimes detained; but an official party like Takasue's obviously had no difficulty in crossing.

33. Until 1708 Mount Fuji was an active volcano.

34. Kiyomi Barrier: near the modern city of Shizuoka.

35. Ōi River, which formed the border between Suruga and Tōtōmi Provinces, flows into Suruga Bay near modern Kawasaki. As will be seen from map 1, the author has totally confused the sequence of Kiyomi, Tagonaura, Ōi River, and Fuji River. This is not surprising if she was writing some thirty years after the events described (see introduction, page 17).

36. List of Appointments: from the ninth to the eleventh of the First

Month an official list was issued announcing the main appointments to provincial posts. The list of Imperial appointments (including governorships) was written on yellow paper; lower appointments were on white paper.

37. Saya no Nakayama: one of the most famous mountain passes on the Tōkaidō. It figures frequently in classical poetry, and a young Heian lady would have to be extremely ill not to notice it.

38. Tenchū River: probably refers to Tenryū River in modern Shizuoka Prefecture. Lady Sarashina was lodged in a separate building to protect the other members of the party from the ritual defilement caused by the proximity of illness (see note 10).

39. Hamana Ko is a famous lagoon in western Shizuoka (map 1); an inlet called Imagire leads directly to the ocean. It is now a popular sightseeing resort and every weekend thousands of motorists converge on the vast *doraivin* (drive-in) beside the lagoon to sample such local delicacies as *karēraisu* (curry-rice) and to admire what can be seen of the lagoon through the almost solid mass of human bodies and the haze of exhaust fumes.

40. Lady Sarashina has in mind the famous poem,

> *Sooner will the waves cover the pines of Sue no Matsuyama*
> *Than I falseheartedly forsake you*

Sue no Matsuyama, in the northern territory of Mutsu, was much mentioned by poets; it lay far from the sea.

41. December in the Western calendar.

42. Reference to a poem by Lady Nakatsukasa,

> *Cross it, and trouble lies ahead.*
> *Do not cross, and still you're trouble-bound.*
> *Truly a troublous place*
> *Is the Ford of Shikasuga.*

Lady Sarashina has made a mistake about this ford: Shikasuga, being within Mikawa Province near Takashi Beach, was not on the border of Owari Province.

43. Probably a friend of the author's father. He belonged to an ancient Ōmi family and may have had Imperial connexions.

44. The "Lake" always referred to Lake Biwa, the huge lute-shaped lake northeast of the Capital.

45. The Barrier was Ōsaka Barrier on the border of Yamashiro and Ōmi Provinces (map 1). Travellers in the Heian period who were returning from a long journey normally planned to reach their destination after nightfall. According to Professor Miyata (SNHyo, p. 94), this was so that people would not see how exhausted they looked.

46. Sanjō Palace in the Third Ward of the Capital (map 2) was the residence of Princess Osako (Shūshi Naishinnō, 996–1049), the daughter of Emperor Ichijō and Empress Sadako. One of the author's relations served in the Palace as a lady-in-waiting. Professor Tsunoda has identified the exact site of Takasue's palace (see Tsunoda Bunei, "Sugawara no Takasue no Teitaku" in *Kodai Bunka*, xv, no. 1 (1965).

47. Lids of boxes were frequently used for carrying or sending books, clothes, etc. Often the receptacles were not actual lids but containers made to look like lids.

48. To accompany her husband, Lady Sarashina's father, when he went to Kazusa in 1017. "Had been going through a difficult time": lit. "there had been various things that were not as she had thought." This is a typical euphemism for "was not getting on with her husband." For the relative flexibility of Heian marriage arrangements see Ivan Morris, "Marriage in the World of Genji," *Asia* (Spring, 1968).

49. The "unawaited" person is Lady Sarashina's real mother, who returned home shortly after the departure of the stepmother. The "plum tree's trailing branch" refers, of course, to Lady Sarashina herself.

50. For this nurse, see p. 43 above.

51. This was the daughter of the famous calligrapher (and close friend of Sei Shōnagon's), Fujiwara no Yukinari (971–1027), who had undoubtedly passed on some of his enthusiasm for calligraphy to his daughter. Her husband was Michinaga's son, Nagaie.

52. First two lines of a poem by Mibu no Tadamine,

Had I not lain awake last night,
I should have heard the hototogisu's *song*
Only through other people's words

(i.e., I would have had to depend on others to tell me about the song).

53. Anonymous. Toribe No was the famous place of cremation east of the Capital (map 2). This evocative site, the supreme symbol of transience in Heian Japan, has now almost completely disappeared owing to the construction of the new superhighway to Nagoya.

54. Lady Sarashina refers to *Waka Murasaki* (Chapter 5 of *The Tale of Genji*) and to other early chapters of the novel. In her time the various chapters or books (*kan*) of the great novel were bound and distributed separately.

55. "Mother" is presumably her real parent, as opposed to the stepmother of the previous section (note 49).
Uzumasa is the site of Kōryū Ji, the famous Shingon temple to the west of the Capital (PBk, note 920).

56. *Zai* is probably *Ise Monogatari* (note 24). The other books are all unknown, being among the innumerable Heian works of fiction that have disappeared. This passage contains the first extant reference to *The Tale of Genji* as having about fifty chapters; the exact length is fifty-four, of which Arthur Waley translated fifty-three.

57. My curtain: *kichō*—curtain of state or curtain-frame, a piece of furniture that played a most important part in Heian domestic architecture. It was a portable frame, about six feet high and of variable width, which supported opaque hangings and was mainly aimed at protecting the women of the house from being seen by men and strangers. Heian women of the upper class spent a good part of their time behind these curtains, a sort of *purdah*.

58. Yūgao was Genji's beautiful young mistress who died, bewitched by the jealous spirit of Lady Rokujō. Ukifune, the heroine of the final books of *The Tale of Genji*, was the mistress of both Kaoru ("the Captain of Uji") and Prince Niou; torn between her affection for these two young noblemen, she tried to drown herself in Uji River, but

was rescued and became a nun at the age of twenty-one. Both heroines came from a far humbler class than the men, and both their young lives were marked by the type of romantic tragedy that obviously appealed to Lady Sarashina (see Introduction, pp. 20–21).

59. See p. 47 above.

60. There is a conventional play of words on *aki*—(i) autumn, (ii) (world-) weary.

61. The Empress Dowager was Fujiwara no Michinaga's daughter, Kazuko, the consort of Emperor Sanjō. Her daughter, the Imperial Princess Teishi, usually known as Yōmeimon In, belonged to the first of the four Imperial Orders. The Hall of Six Sides was part of Chōbō Temple of the Tendai Sect, and the Princess (now aged nine) had evidently ordered the man in Lady Sarashina's dream to build an artificial stream in the garden as her contribution to the temple.

62. That is, to the Sun Goddess, the patron Shinto deity of the Imperial family. Lady Sarashina's dream does not seem to make much sense—but nor do most people's dreams. For the significance of these dreams see Introduction, pp. 21–22.

63. For detailed explanations about the avoidance of unlucky directions and its great importance in Heian life, see WSP, pp. 137–39, and PBk, note 103.

64. Would eat only the daintiest food: in other words, it was a "good" cat. For Heian ideas about social classes see WSP, pp. 81–84; about cats see PBk, note 44; about dreams see WSP, pp. 141–42. This was a female cat.

65. Northern wing: i.e., the dark, less attractive part of the house where the servants lived. Later the term came to designate the servants' quarters regardless of geographical position.

66. *Ch'ang Hên Ko* (*Chōgonka*) by Po Chü-i (772–846), probably the most popular Chinese poem in Japan during the Heian period. It tells the story of the tragic love between the Chinese Emperor and his favourite concubine, the beautiful Yang Kuei-fei, who according to one version was hanged from a pear tree by mutinous troops in 756 owing to her alleged responsibility for the Emperor's neglect of state

affairs and to the unpopularity of her scheming family. We know from *The Tale of Genji* that this famous poem had been rewritten in the phonetic Japanese syllabary and was much read in Court circles as an illustrated Tale, but this version had already been lost by the fifteenth century.

67. The seventh day of the Seventh Month: the day of the Weaver Festival, which is derived from a Chinese legend about the love of the Weaver and the Herdsman, represented by the stars Vega and Altair respectively. Because of her love for the Herdsman, the Weaver neglected her work on the clothes for the gods, while the Herdsman neglected his cattle. As a punishment the Heavenly Emperor put the two stars on opposite sides of the Milky Way, decreeing that they should be allowed to meet only once a year, on the seventh day of the Seventh Month, when a company of heavenly magpies use their wings to form a bridge that the Weaver can cross to join her lover. The seventh day of the Seventh Month is of course associated with romantic love (something like St. Valentine's Day), and it is mentioned towards the end of Po Chü-i's famous poem in the passage that describes the return to earth of the Taoist priest who has visited Yang Kuei-fei in the abode of the dead. The translation is by Witter Bynner:

> *And she sent him, by his messenger, a sentence reminding him of vows*
> *which had been known only to their two hearts:*
> *"On the seventh day of the Seventh-month, in the Palace of Long Life,*
> *We told each other secretly in the quiet midnight world*
> *That we wished to fly in heaven, two birds with the wings of one,*
> *And to grow together on the earth, two branches of one tree"*
> *. . . Earth endures, heaven endures; sometimes both shall end,*
> *While this unending sorrow goes on and on forever.**

The last line of Lady Sarashina's poem is an implied request to be lent the Tale version of *The Song of Everlasting Regret. Namiutsu* means (i) to beat, surge (of waves), (ii) to surge (of a yearning in one's heart). The owner's reply suggests that normally *The Song of Everlasting*

---

* Cyril Birch, ed., *Anthology of Chinese Literature* (New York: Grove Press, 1965), p. 269.

Regret would be a sad, ill-omened poem that one would hesitate to give to anyone, but that on this particular day, when the Herdsman and the Weaver (and, by implication, other lovers like Yang Kuei-fei and her Emperor) can meet, the inauspicious nature of the poem is forgotten and so there is no objection to lending it to Lady Sarashina.

68. The name of a woman, presumably the mistress of the man in the carriage.

69. For the irregularity of Heian bedtimes see WSP, pp. 161–62.

70. The present passage contains the only original reference to this curiously entitled book.

71. The nurse's reply-poem is an ingenious web of puns, pivot-words, and the like. Grief was no obstacle to poetic dexterity; on the contrary poetry alone was capable of expressing the full extent of a person's sorrow.

72. The vanishing smoke from a cremated body was a standard image of evanescence and of death's finality. The nurse's visit to the crematory at Toribe No (note 53) is the subject of this and the next three poems, which all ring the changes on the theme of the smoke that rose from the sister's cremated body—smoke that soon disappeared, leaving no guide to help the nurse find the grave.

73. Yoshino (map 1) was a mountainous region some sixty miles south of Heian Kyō; it was noted for its heavy snowfalls. The nun was probably an acquaintance or relation of Lady Sarashina's.

74. For the excitements and disappointments attending these annual promotions see *The Pillow Book of Sei Shōnagon*, Vol. I, pp. 3–4 and 22–23.

75. I have tried to suggest the play of words on *naru:* (i) the bell rings; (ii) one's ambitions are realized, by a clumsy pun on "toll."

76. Eastern Hills, Higashiyama, a hilly district just east of the Capital; now it is a suburb of Kyoto, but in 1024 it was open country.

77. I.e., "Do you really think you can deceive me with your tapping sound? I know perfectly well that no one will be visiting me here."

The water-rail (*kuina, rallus aquaticus indicus*) was noted for making a tapping sound like a woodpecker.

78. Ryōzen: one of the 36 Peaks of Higashiyama and the site of a well-known temple (map 2).

79. Both Lady Sarashina and her companion have in mind a tenth-century love poem by Ki no Tsurayuki:

> *Scooping the water in my hands, I muddied the shallow mountain well*
> *And could not slake my thirst.*
> *So now I'm forced to part from her I love*
> *And cannot stay to drink my fill.*

The well in Tsurayuki's poem was so shallow that just a few drops from the hands of the person who was scooping it up were enough to stir the mud at the bottom and to make the water undrinkable. Lady Sarashina's poem is in the form of a rhetorical question ("Have you only just now realized . . . ?") and there is a pun on *nomi:* (i) only, (ii) drink.

80. "Invoking the Sacred Name" (*Nembutsu*) refers to the increasingly popular practice in Heian Buddhism of meditating on the name of Amida Buddha and intoning the formula, "I call on thee, Amida Buddha" (Namu Amida Butsu). This was to become the basis of popular Buddhism in succeeding centuries.

81. *Hototogisu:* usually translated as "cuckoo"; but the *hototogisu (cuculus poliocephalus)* is a far more poetic type of bird with none of the cuckoo's cheeky associations, and I prefer to leave it in the original. The name *hototogisu* is an onomatopoeia derived from the bird's characteristic cry of *ho-to-to*. "Wood thrush" is also sometimes given as a translation of *hototogisu*, but ornithologically it is at least as inaccurate as "cuckoo."

82. The poem lends itself to several alternative or simultaneous interpretations, depending on the many possible meanings of *shiranedomo* ("even though I/he/one do/does not know"). E.g. (i) one cannot tell about moonlit nights, which may be distracting, but on ordinary

nights someone would certainly be thinking about us; (ii) even people who are unfamiliar with mountain villages would think of us on such a night; (iii) I don't know about other people, but I know that *I* always think about mountain villages on such occasions.

83. "Yet you, a fellow human being, have left without even coming to see me" is implied.

84. This is regarded as one of Lady Sarashina's finest and most characteristic poems, and it is included in many anthologies. More literally it goes, "Night after night as I lie here listening to the rustling of the bamboo leaves, I am overcome by an undefinable sadness."

85. "Dew" refers to her hosts' hospitality, and "plain of reeds" is the house where she stayed. Lady Sarashina implies that, though she is receiving ample hospitality from her new hosts, she thinks with special gratitude of the hospitality in the house by the bamboo grove. A typical Heian "thank-you note."

86. Heian ladies were frequently named after the official posts that their husbands, brothers, and so on held in the central government or in the provinces. When Lady Sarashina's stepmother resumed Court service after returning from the province of Kazusa (p. 53 above), she continued to be known as Kazusa-dayū (the Senior Assistant Minister from Kazusa) because of her husband's former post in that province. She kept the name even after she was separated from this husband (Lady Sarashina's father) and acquired a new husband, in the same way that women in the West who have been married to titled men retain their husband's title even when they have been divorced. "Acquired a new husband" refers to the uxorilocal Heian custom according to which the wife continued to live in her own home and "had her husband visit her" there (see note 48).

87. Lady Sarashina's poem is ingeniously based on one by Emperor Tenji (seventh century) that later became a famous folk-song. "Dwell among the clouds" was a standard image for life at Court. To write a poem for a friend or relations was standard Heian practice and did not imply that the other person was incapable of writing his or her own poem.

88. Or, according to another possible interpretation, "I could not pray that I might become like other people."

89. In the Second Month of 1032 Sugawara no Takasue was appointed Assistant Governor of Hitachi, one of the Great Provinces in the east of Japan (PBk, note 324). The Governor of this province was usually an Imperial Prince, and Takasue's post was the highest one available there for a commoner. A note in the original Teika manuscript informs us that in this year he was fifty-nine and his daughter twenty-four.

90. That is, in 1017 to the province of Kazusa when she was nine years old. The doleful plight of girls who have grown up in distant provinces will be familiar to all readers of *The Tale of Genji* (e.g., WSP, p. 96). Going to seed alone in the Capital was a wretched fate, but not nearly so bad as vegetating in the provinces and becoming a "country person" (*inakabito*). On the whole the complaint of Lady Sarashina's father seems as desultory and confused in the original Japanese as in my translation.

91. The time has now come for her to get married, and the chances of making a good match were drastically reduced by a recent connexion with the provinces.

92. Pocket-paper: elegant coloured paper that gentlemen carried in the folds of their clothes. It served for writing notes and poems, as well as for more corporeal purposes.

93. Literally, "If I were a person for whom things went as I wished, I should have known Autumn parting deeply." In classical Japanese literature Autumn was the traditional season for partings, and "Autumn parting" was a set phrase in poetry. Lady Sarashina's father complains that he cannot even have a proper "Autumn parting."

94. "Not much good at poetry": more literally, "The poems I put together were loin-broken." This conventional expression of modesty need not be taken any more seriously than those of the modern Japanese tycoon who refers to his "rapidly failing concern" and informs his dinner guests that there is nothing to eat.

95. For Uzumasa, see note 55.

96. The gentleman's message consists of the last two lines of a thirty-one-syllable poem. As convention demanded, Lady Sarashina's reply gives the first three lines of 5, 7, and 5 syllables respectively. Her smug implication is that flighty, elegant gentlemen who are concerned with a variety of worldly affairs would naturally assume that a serious woman like herself, who is in fact bound on a pilgrimage, must be going on a mere flower-viewing expedition. This is the sort of *badinage* in which Sei Shōnagon excelled.

97. I.e., "how fondly they must be recalling the peaceful Autumn season when they were at their height!" Lady Sarashina refers of course to her recollections of the happy time before her father left for Hitachi. The plant in question is *hagi* or bush-clover (*lespedeza bicolor*).

98. It was customary for a newly appointed Governor to make an official circuit of the principal Shinto shrines in his province.

99. This appears to be a sentimental conceit by Lady Sarashina's father. The village in question is almost certainly Oshinobe in Ibaraki District (Province of Hitachi). He changes it to Koshinobi, which means "longing for one's child."

100. Mount Chichibu (in Musashi near her father's new province) is introduced exclusively for the element *chichi*, which means "father." Far-fetched puns on place names were a standard ingredient of elegant poetry.

101. Lady Sarashina was now about twenty-seven—old enough, one would imagine, to go on short pilgrimages by herself. Hase was a famous eighth-century temple of the Shingon sect; it was situated south of Nara (map 2) and dedicated to the eleven-faced Bodhisattva Kannon, the Goddess of Mercy (see photograph, p. 100). Nara Slope (also known as the Slope of Tortures) was to the north of Nara, the great temple centre. It was in Ishiyama Temple on the shore of Lake Biwa (photographs, p. 97) that Lady Murasaki was traditionally believed to have started *The Tale of Genji*. Kurama: Shingon temple in the mountains some seven miles north of the Capital (photographs, pp. 110-111). Kiyomizu: established in 805 in honour of the Eleven-Faced Kannon. It is situated about halfway up Otowa Yama, a slope

in the east of the Capital; the main temple stands on a cliff with a famous wooden platform in front (photographs, p. 77).

102. The Equinox (Higan, Paramitā): two important weeks for Buddhist observances following the Spring and Autumn equinoxes respectively.

103. Curtained enclosure by the altar: literally, "inside the dog-barrier." Low, latticed screens separating the inner part of the temple from the outer; derived from the barriers placed at the foot of the steps leading up to private mansions in order to keep out stray dogs. Intendant: priest in charge of an important temple like Tōdai in Nara or Kiyomizu outside the Capital, where he served as an official representative of the Imperial government.

104. For abstinence, see note 164 and PBk, note 31. The mother's rather abrupt way of addressing the priest may seem surprising, but we should remember (a) her own distinguished antecedents (Introduction, p. 13); (b) the low social status of most Heian priests ("...most people are convinced that a priest is as unimportant as a piece of wood, and they treat him accordingly," writes Sei Shōnagon in *The Pillow Book.*

105. It was fashionable for women to let the bottom of their many-layered costume protrude outside their curtain of state or from the carriage in which they were travelling so that visitors might admire the colour combination.

106. It is not clear who gave her this repeated (*tsune ni*) advice; probably it was someone in a dream, since the wording is almost identical with that on page 57, above. Here Lady Sarashina emphasizes her almost total indifference to established religions by pretending that she did not even know whether the Sun Goddess was a sort of female Buddha or a Shinto deity.

107. Ise, about seventy-miles from the Capital, was (and still is) the site of the most important Shinto shrines in Japan. Sacred mirrors were enshrined as symbols of the Sun Goddess in both the Great Ise Shrine and the Hinokuma-Kunikakasu Shrine in nearby Kii Province. The latter was under the protection of the Provincial Chieftain of Kii.

This was originally the rank of the chief provincial official, but after the Great Reform in the seventh century it became an honorary title involving only religious duties such as worshipping the sacred mirror. Still another mirror was enshrined in the Ummei Hall in the Imperial Palace in the Capital (map 3), where it was kept in the Sacred Mirror Room and zealously guarded by Palace Attendants. The Mirror was one of the Three Imperial Regalia (the other two are the Sword and the Jewel), and was central to official Shinto worship. Since Lady Sarashina was unable to worship the terrestrial symbols of the Sun Goddess, it occurred to her that she could very well worship the "light in heaven," that, is, the sun itself. For a brief discussion of Shintoism as sun worship see D. C. Holtom, *Modern Japan and Shinto Nationalism* (Cambridge, Eng.: Cambridge University Press; Chicago, University of Chicago Press, 1947), pp. 64–65.

108. Shugaku Temple: in the western foothills of Mount Hiei, a few miles northeast of the Capital (map 2).

109. The nun's reply evidently implies that her own emotions are as dense as the foliage of the trees leading to Mount Hiei in the summer; but the poem is unusually obscure, and one possible interpretation is that the dense summer foliage refers to the writer's confused state of mind *before* she entered the temple.

110. Western Hills: from later references it appears that the house was in Kadono District not far from Ninna Temple, some five miles from the centre of the Capital.

111. See page 73, above. Takasue's reference to Fate echoes the lament in his poem written when he was leaving for the East.

112. The theme of renunciation and its devastating effect on those who are left behind is common in classical Japanese Literature. Cf. WSP, pp. 132–33.

113. Mount Hiei: mountain range northeast of the Capital, headquarters of the Tendai sect of Buddhism; Inari Shrines: a group of three Shinto shrines built in 711 on the slopes of a hill a couple of miles south of the Capital; Narabi Hills: a pair of hills in Kadono District, a few miles

south of where the author now lived. For the entire scene see map 2.

114. "Rice fields" (*ta to iu mono*—"things called rice fields"), is a typical affectation of a well-born young Heian woman who wishes to suggest her unfamiliarity with such inelegant, countrified things as rice fields even though they were the primary source of her physical and aesthetic pabulum (cf. PBk, note 461, where Sei Shōnagon speaks of "what I took to be rice plants"). Bird-clappers, on the other hand. had attractive poetic associations.

115. I.e., the wind is less forgetful than old friends: a common theme in Heian poetry (cf. note 83).

116. Invited to attend Court: as a lady-in-waiting to Princess Yūshi (1038–1105), the third daughter of the reigning emperor, Gosuzaku. Her mother, Empress Genshi, died in 1039 and we know that Lady Sarashina did not enter her service until after the mother's death. The probable date is the winter of 1039, when Princess Yūshi was one year old and Lady Sarashina thirty-one. The Princess's residence was Takakura Palace, which belonged to the Chancellor, Fujiwara no Yorimichi (who was her mother's adoptive father). Takakura was a Detached Palace (i.e., an Imperial residence outside the actual Imperial compound), and was situated directly to the east of the main palace buildings. Princess Yūshi had been born in this residence and was consequently called Princess Takakura.

117. For court ladies' dresses see WSP, pp. 206, 216–17, etc., and PBk, App.8*a*.

118. This (*ikaga semu*) and similar phrases of Buddhist resignation are common in Lady Sarashina's writing; they occur only rarely in *The Pillow Book.*

119. Concerning eavesdroppers and Peeping Toms see WSP, pp. 50, 180.

120. The usual absence of pronouns makes it unclear who is saying this. Most of the commentaries suggest that it is her mother *and* father, but obviously Lady Sarashina's parents are not speaking in a chorus. Her father is probably the principal speaker, while her mother chimes in with an occasional whine.

121. Difference: the Japanese word is *nioi*, which here means "virtue" in the sense of "power to attract people."

122. Intendant: see note 103, above. For Kiyomizu, see note 101.

123. Much better family: that is, into the Sugawara family (see Introduction, p. 13). A carver of Buddhist images was a mere artisan and therefore far lower in the Heian scale than any "good person" (WSP, p. 320).

124. Naming of the Buddhas: One of the last of the annual ceremonies, it was celebrated in the various palaces towards the end of the Twelfth Month. The services were aimed at expunging the sins one had committed during the course of the year.

125. From the old poem,

> *As sunk in doleful thoughts*
> *I wearily await my love,*
> *Even the moon's face reflected on my sleeves*
> *Is wet with tears.*

126. Everything is coming to an end: the closing year, the night, the moonlight—all are equally evanescent.

127. Picked the parsley: for the origin of this peculiar phrase, see PBk, note 136. Here it refers to a situation in which, despite one's best efforts, things do not turn out as one had hoped.

128. From here until ". . . Goddess Herself" (top of page 89) the original Japanese consists of a single sentence, many parts of which are extremely obscure.

129. Cf. note 58. Uji was a village some 10 miles south of the Capital where Ukifune lived in a gloomy house by the river and was visited secretly by her two lovers. This house, which is the main setting for the later chapters of Murasaki's novel, belonged to Ukifune's father (and Genji's half-brother), Prince Hachi. The old prince lived there alone with his two elder daughters; after his death Ukifune moved in with her attendants.

130. In the Fourth month of 1042, when the Princess was four years old,

she was taken for a visit from Takakura Palace (note 116) to the Imperial Palace compound in the company of her ladies-in-waiting, including Lady Sarashina.

131. See notes 62 and 107.

132. Lady Hakase: literally her name means something like "Lady Professor." Probably her father or other close relation was a Doctor of Literature (cf. note 86). This venerable old lady served in the Sacred Mirror Room (note 107).

133. Lit. "Wistaria Tub Palace." Many of the Palace buildings, especially those used by women, were named after the flowering shrubs planted in tubs outside.

Lady Umetsubo: this was Fujiwara no Norimichi's daughter, Nariko (d.1068), one of the principal concubines of the reigning emperor, Gosuzaku. Like most Imperial consorts she was named after the building in the Imperial Palace compound where she resided. She was now on her way to spend the night with the Emperor in his residence, Seiryō Palace, which was a few hundred yards to the south.

134. The speaker refers to Princess Yūshi's mother (note 116), who had died three years earlier.

135. "Heavenly Door" is the sliding-door through which Lady Umetsubo enters on her visit to the Emperor. The poem centres on the image of "dwelling among the clouds" (note 87), which is related to "heavenly door" and "moon." Though an outsider to the Palace, Lady Sarashina is overcome by nostalgia at the thought of the dead Empress whose place has now been taken by a new consort; like the moon above, she sadly surveys the scene.

136. The Chancellor: Fujiwara no Yorimichi, who was Chancellor (WSP, p. 319) from 1020 to 1068. He lived in Kaya Palace, directly opposite Takakura Palace; both residences belonged to him.

137. A poetic way of saying that the memory of their conversation is still fresh in her mind.

138. The other Court lady suggests that she deserves more pity than Lady Sarashina; for she is on duty every night and never has a chance to sleep soundly.

139. Reeds: "Japanese pampas grass," says the Kenkyūsha Dictionary, but the phrase (like so many other botanical and ornithological ones in the Japanese-English dictionary) appears to have been invented especially for the occasion. The technical equivalent of susuki is *miscanthus sinensis* or *eularia japonica*.

140. High Court Nobles: a designation for all gentlemen of the Third Rank and above, as well as for Imperial Advisers of the Fourth Rank.

   Senior Courtiers: gentlemen of the Fourth or Fifth Rank who had the privilege of waiting in attendance on the Emperor in the Senior Courtiers' Chamber. For the rank system see WSP, pp. 78–82, and PBk, p. 237.

141. Perpetual Sacred Readings: held at irregular intervals in the Palace. Readings of various sutras would continue day and night, each priest (in a group of twelve) reading for about two hours at a time. The date of the present scene is 1042, when the writer was thirty-three years old.

142. This gentleman was Minamoto no Sukemichi (1005–1060), the Controller of the Right and a respected poet, who later became an Imperial Adviser and rose to the Second Rank. In the present scene he is thirty-seven years old; he belongs to the Fourth Rank and is far too grand to be greeted by ordinary Court ladies like Sarashina. Sukemichi's family had a long tradition of musical accomplishment and he himself was a distinguished performer; this interest is reflected in his discussion of the seasons.

143. He showed his true sensitivity by evoking *mono no aware* (the pathos of things, *lacrimae rerum*, see WSP, pp. 318–19). This and poetic skill were the surest ways to the heart of a shy young Heian lady.

144. As usual in situations of this kind, the ladies can be heard but not seen. Lady Sarashina never actually sees Sukemichi; hence the importance that she attaches to the tone of his voice.

145. Comparisons of the charms of Spring and Autumn, traditionally the two favourite seasons in Japan, occur frequently in classical poetry and fiction; see, for example, the famous opening passage of *The Pillow Book*. By embarking on such a comparison Sukemichi consolidates

the favourable impression he has already made on Lady Sarashina and her companion.

146. Fragrant Breeze: the Fuga was regarded as the basic key of the twenty-six keys of the *biwa* lute.

147. Another of Lady Sarashina's most respected poems; it is included in the famous *Shinkokin Shū* anthology of 1201. A more literal translation would be, "The hazy-looking moon on Spring nights when both the light green sky and the cherry blossoms are all wrapped uniformly by the mist."

148. Sukemichi's suggestion that his life might come to an end at any moment is not to be taken literally; this was simply a conventional expression of *mujōkan* (the sense of impermanence) (WSP, p. 323); in fact he lived another eighteen years.

149. A literal line-by-line translation would be,

> *People all*
> *To Spring their hearts*
> *Seem to have drawn*
> *Shall I alone (indeed) see*
> *The moon on the Autumn night?*

150. For instance in *The Tale of Genji* and *The Pillow Book*. The following typical passage is from *Agemaki* (Book 47) of *The Tale of Genji*: "The Twelfth Month moon, which people have always been said to regard as a depressing thing, now emerged in a cloudless sky . . . "

151. The formal donning of a ceremonial skirt was central to the coming-of-age ritual for girls. In 1025 Sukemichi, who was then a Chamberlain, travelled to the Great Ise Shrine to present the skirt and other accoutrements from the Court to the High Priestess, Princess Yoshiko, the daughter of Prince Tomohira, who served as High Priestess from 1018 to 1036.

152. Enyū reigned from 969 to 984, so these attendants had been in Ise for about forty years, during which time they had served five successive High Priestesses.

153. Senior Courtier: see note 140. The Senior Courtiers' Chamber was a room in the south of the Emperor's residential palace, Seiryō Den,

used only by courtiers who were specially permitted to wait in attendance on the Emperor.

154. Most of the ladies-in-waiting occupied rooms off the long, narrow corridors on both sides of the Palace buildings and in the rear.

155. Creep out: the traditional Japanese seating position is a sort of squat; if one was seated and wished to move to a place nearby, one would normally go on one's knees, rather than stand up and kneel down again in the new place.

156. Commentators differ about this passage. According to some, it means that Sukemichi also realized that the evening was unsuitable for a meeting because there were so many people about; another interpretation is that Sukemichi, like Lady Sarashina, thought that this would be a perfect evening for the promised flute-playing. The ambiguity, like so many in classical Japanese, is probably deliberate.

157. More literally, "Did you know the feelings of me who, awaiting a moment when no one was there, rowed out to Kashima on the Bay of Naruto, oh fisherman of the seashore?" Lady Sarashina's poem is an ingenious tangle of puns, pivot words, etc. For instance, the *ma* in Kashi*ma* refers to the "moment" when she can creep out of her room unnoticed and *to* in Naru*to* refers to the door of her room. (*Kashima* may also imply *kashimashi*, "noisy, boisterous," in reference to the commotion in the Palace that prevented their meeting.) *Kogare* in *kogareiuru* ("row") has the additional sense of "burning" or "longing" for someone. The fisherman, of course, is Sukemichi. We do not know whether he ever saw this passionate poem. Probably he did not, since there is no record of any reply. Sukemichi was far too much of a gentleman to commit such a solecism as leaving a poem unanswered, and surely Lady Sarashina would have included the answer in her book.

158. Following the abortive romance with Sukemichi there is a gap of about eighteen months in the narrative. During this time Lady Sarashina was married to Tachibana no Toshimichi (1002–1058), a gentleman of the provincial governor class. His father, Tameyoshi, had been Governor of Tajima Province, and he himself was subsequently appointed to the governorship of Shimotsuke and Shinano. She had

also had a boy, Tadatoshi, the "bud" to whom she refers in this passage; later she had one more son and a daughter.

. . . both in social standing and in material wealth": literally the passage means, "Having reached a state of abundant force . . . and having myself accumulated treasures as high as Mount Mikura." This is something of a hyperbole; there is no evidence that Toshimichi was powerful or rich. Mount Mikura contains a pun on *kura* (the storehouse where valuables were kept). For Ishiyama Temple see note 101.

159. See p. 52, above. The previous visit had been twenty-five years earlier when Lady Sarashina was travelling to the Capital for the first time.

160. Seki Temple (The Temple of the Barrier) had been built towards the end of the eighth century on the site where the city of Ōtsu now stands. The huge statue of Buddha that impressed Lady Sarashina so greatly on her previous visit belonged to this temple. When she first saw the temple, it had been under reconstruction.

161. (a) The beach had not changed, but (b) what great changes had taken place in me since I last saw it! The idea implied in (b) would come immediately to the mind of any Heian reader; for this was a standard theme in classical poetry.

162. For bathing and its ritual significance see WSP, p. 157. The characters with which "bath house" *(yuya)* is usually written mean "house of purification." Lady Sarashina and her companion go *down* to the bath house but *up* to the temple itself.

163. The Great Festival of Thanksgiving, one of the most important and impressive Shinto celebrations, took place towards the beginning of each new Imperial Reign. It corresponded to the annual Festival of the First Fruits (WSP, p. 177), in which the Emperor offered newly harvested rice to Amaterasu and the other Shinto deities and then partook of new rice himself. The Festival was preceded by a Sacred Purification; this was a magnificent ceremony in which the emperor performed ritual ablution by the waters of the Kamo River. The present Festival marked the accession of Emperor Goreizei in 1045. The Great Thanksgiving Festival took place in the Eleventh Month and the Sacred Purification in the middle of the Tenth Month.

164. For Hase Temple see note 101 and map 2. Before going on pilgrimages it was customary to purify oneself by ritual ablutions, abstention from meat, fish, and other forbidden food, and by refraining from sexual intercourse.

165. My husband: literally, "the man who was the father of my child," i.e., Toshimichi (note 158). This rather circumlocutory way of identifying her husband does not mean that Lady Sarashina enjoyed mystifications of the "one Abyssinian is the father of the other Abyssinian's son" variety; rather it comes from a traditional reluctance to give specific names or identifications to people, even to those who are closest to one. Thus Lady Sarashina would never refer to her father as "Father" or by his name, Sugawara no Takasue, but by some such vague phrase as "the person who was my parent" (*oya naru hito*).

166. Galleries: elaborate grandstands, complete with screens, curtains, etc., built for viewing Imperial processions and other outdoor ceremonies.

167. The grandson of the former Chancellor, Fujiwara no Michitaka. His mansion was 200 yards northwest of Sanjō Palace.

168. The original text has the rather charming idiom, "What good does it do to fatten one's eyes temporarily?" i.e., to feast one's eyes on something that will give no lasting nourishment. It is tempting to retain such exoticisms in a translation—tempting but unwise.

169. Hōsō Temple: tenth-century temple built by Fujiwara no Tadahira south of the Capital (map 2).

170. Uji: see notes 58 and 129.

171. Among "Trivial Things that Become Important on Special Occasions" Sei Shōnagon lists "The boatman when one is crossing on a ferry."

172. The Chancellor's villa: this was originally an Imperial villa dating from the tenth century. In 998 it was acquired by the great Fujiwara no Michinaga, and in 1046, the date of the present visit, it was the residence of his son, Yorimichi, the ruling Chancellor. Six years later it was reconstructed as a temple, the magnificent Byōdō In (map 2 and photograph, p. 105), which is one of the few buildings still left

from the Heian period. Presumably Lady Sarashina was able to enter the villa as lady-in-waiting to Yorimichi's granddaughter, Princess Yūshi (note 116). Prince Hachi's house in Uji (note 129) must have been incomparably more austere than Yorimichi's grand residence; but Lady Sarashina tended to glamourize the world of fiction.

173. Mount Kurikoma: mountain about one mile southwest of Uji Bridge (map 2); apparently it was infested with highway robbers. Readers of *The Tale of Genji* will recall Kaoru's fear of being attacked by highwaymen when he visited Uji.

174. According to some commentators, "our things" (*chōdo*) refers to bows and arrows; but it seems unlikely that a group of pilgrims travelling from the Capital to Nara in 1046 would be armed.

175. "It's hard to find anywhere suitable in these parts": literally, "The place is halfway/awkward," i.e., it was a considerable distance from any posting-station on the road between Nara and the Capital.

176. One of my women: literally "the women who were in the rear part," i.e., low-ranking female servants who stayed in the back of the house to keep watch.

177. Tōdai Temple: the great fane of the Kegon Sect just outside Nara (map 2); it was built by Emperor Shōmu in the middle of the eighth century and occupied a central position in the Buddhist hierarchy of temples as the clan temple of the Imperial family.

178. The Shinto shrine of Isonokami was situated in the village of Furu about five miles south of Nara (map 2). By a typical pun it came to be known as "the Ancient" because *furu*, written with a different character, means "old."

179. Lady Hakase: see note 132.

180. The Inari Shrines (note 113) were dedicated to the gods of the five grains. Pilgrims used to pick branches of *sugi* (cryptomeria) which grew near the shrines and wear them on their headdress to show that they had made the auspicious visit. The longer the *sugi* remained unwithered, the more efficacious the pilgrimage was supposed to have been. It was typical of Heian eclecticism that during a retreat in

a Buddhist temple Lady Sarashina should have dreamt about an auspicious offering from a distant Shinto shrine (see WSP, p. 106). Many years later, after her husband's death, she bitterly regretted that she had not visited the shrines on her return to the Capital (see p. 119).

181. Nara Slope: see note 101.

182. Kurama: see note 101.

183. According to Heian beliefs, it was dew and autumn rains that turned maple leaves red.

184. Poems based on mistaken visual or auditory impressions were especially popular; the most common were those in which cherry blossoms are mistaken for snow or vice-versa, a convention that seemed to have inexhaustible fascination for Heian poetasters.

185. For the efficacy of the *sugi*, see note 180.

186. Leather leg-pieces: wide leather coverings tied round the waist and worn over the front of the legs while riding.

187. This famous poem, which is included in several anthologies, is peculiarly intractable to translation. Literally it means something like "Even in the sky on an aimless journey what accompanies one without staying behind is the dawn moon on which I gazed in the Capital."

188. More literally, "prayed the person on whom I depended would have other people's kind of joy"—a typical series of circumlocutions (cf. note 165).

189. Literally, "Can the affection/flame in the pebbles under the snow of Mount Shira ("White Mountain") be extinguished?" The reply-poem repeats Lady Sarashina's pun on *hi* ("fire") and omo*hi* ("affection, liking"). For Shirayama and Koshi see PBk, note 377.

190. Literally, "Because they grow in the recesses of the hills so far from human habitation, no one comes flower-viewing."

191. Literally, "when the world seemed difficult," a standard euphemism for marital discord (cf. note 48). For Uzumasa see notes 55 and 95.

192. The author compares herself to a woman diver (cf. PBk, notes 363

and 1086). The central image is that of plunging into the rough sea, which in the present context obviously refers to the perils of Court life that the three women had shared in the past. "Wet sleeves" is the limp old image for sorrow. The first reply has a pun on *kai*, which can mean both "shell" and "good effect, usefulness": despite all their efforts to serve effectively at Court, they have incurred nothing but sorrows. The second reply has a pun on *mirume* meaning (i) a type of seaweed that women divers collected, (ii) eyes that see, i.e., the pleasure of meeting you during the breaks between our Court duties: if it were not for the pleasure of seeing you at Court, I should long since have given up these thankless duties.

193. The absence of personal pronouns makes it impossible to tell whether this person (*hito*) is a man or a woman. Professor Miyata suggests that it may be Minamoto no Sukemichi (note 142), for whom Lady Sarashina had felt a romantic attachment ever since her meeting in 1042, and whom she may have continued seeing after her marriage to Tachinana no Toshimichi. The main evidence for this interesting theory is (i) the reference to the moon (see page 93), (ii) the fact that in the Ninth Month of 1050 Sukemichi was appointed to be Senior Assistant Governor-General of the Government Headquarters in Kyushu, which were situated in the province of Chikuzen, (iii) the allusion to a love poem (note 194) that would seem inappropriate if the absent person were a woman. But *kayō ni* ("thus"—"another person" in my translation) surely suggests that Lady Sarashina is in fact writing about another of her female friends, in this case a Court lady whose husband had been appointed to be Governor of Chikuzen and who was leaving the Capital with him for the western provinces.

194. Wished I had never woken up: this refers to a famous love poem by the ninth-century poetess, Ono no Komachi,

> *I fell asleep while he was in my thoughts—*
> *Is that why he appeared before me while I dozed?*
> *Had I but known it was a dream,*
> *I wish that I had never waked.*

195. Yodo: about seven miles south of the Capital (map 2). The border of

Izumi Province was about thirty miles southwest across country; but most of the journey was by boat down the Yodo River, and the travellers spent the night aboard. Takahama was near Naniwa (present-day Osaka). Lady Sarashina's elder brother, Sadayoshi, was Governor of Izumi, and the purpose of her journey was probably to pay him a visit.

196. I.e., from Fuchū, the provincial capital, where Lady Sarashina had been staying. Since the Bay of Ōtsu was only a mile and a half from Fuchū, it might have been more sensible to return there than to wait on the beach for five whole days. But possibly this easy course was precluded by a directional taboo.

197. The poem is elliptical. Some final line like "What then?" must be understood.

198. She was about fifty. The gloomy tone of the present passage contrasts with the optimism on page 96.

199. In 1057 at the age of fifty-five Tachibana no Toshimichi, Lady Sarashina's husband, was appointed to be Governor of Shinano, a large province in the centre of the main island of Japan. Despite its economic and military importance Shinano was too far from the Capital to be regarded as a good post.

200. That is, provinces like Kazusa and Hitachi where Takasue had served as Governor.

201. His daughter: according to Professor Miyata, this was actually Lady Sarashina's own daughter, who had recently been married and who had moved with her husband into a new house. I think it is likelier, however, that it was Toshimichi's daughter with his first wife. If, as seems probable, Lady Sarashina married Toshimichi about 1044, her daughter could not be more than twelve years old at the time of the appointment to Shinano and was unlikely to be married or to have left her parents' house. The actual place of departure was vitally important because of directional taboos; in this case Toshimichi's precautions do not seem to have helped.

202. The lad was called Nakatoshi. We know nothing about him except his official posts, e.g., Assistant Director of the Bureau of Carpentry

(1077), Provisional Governor of Chikugo (1087). We do not know his age when he set off with his father for Shinano, but he was probably not more than twelve.

203. It was believed that a "human fire" or "death fire" (*hitodama*) could be seen leaving the body of someone who was going to die. This fire was usually seen shortly before the person's death; but sometimes it appeared a couple of years in advance. The best way to avert the predicted death was to recite the following formula three times as soon as the death fire appeared: "I have seen a death fire and, though I know not whose death it may betoken, I shall tie up the hem of my skirt." One then tied up the hem of one's skirt (left side for a man, right side for a woman) and let it down again after three days. There is no evidence that this precaution was taken in the present instance.

204. A Governor's normal term of office was four years; it was probably because of ill health that Toshimichi returned to the Capital after less than eight months.

205. Toshimichi was fifty-six and Lady Sarashina fifty.

206. See page 80 above. It will be recalled that the reflexion on the "happy" side of the mirror did not include any human figure.

207. Vanished with the smoke: literally, "made him into clouds and smoke." Owing to Buddhist influence, cremation had become the standard form of disposal in fashionable Heian circles. (see note 53 and WSP, p. 122).

208. It was customary during funerals for close relations of the dead person to wear short white cotton tunics over their black mourning robes. Because of its ominous associations the tunic was thrown away after the ceremony.

209. See p. 104 above.

210. The interpreter: refers to dream interpreters (*yumetoki*, WSP, p. 142). Like modern psychiatrists these interpreters were not always entirely reliable. In this case the first part of their interpretation proved correct since Lady Sarashina did in fact become a nurse to Princess Yūshi (note 116); but the rest was inaccurate, and of course nothing was ever said about the sorrows she could expect in her life.

211. That is, the type of merit or karma that would improve her lot in a future incarnation.

212. Absorbed as ever in her dream world, Lady Sarashina now recalls a religious dream that took place some three years earlier. Her other dreams had proved unreliable (note 210); but for some reason she believed she could depend on this one as a guaranty of ultimate salvation. Amida (Amitâbha), the Buddha of the Western Paradise, had vowed not to enter nirvana himself until every sentient being in the world was saved. According to his Original Vow, all that was needed was to call on Amida by using the Nembutsu formula (note 80); at the believer's death Amida would then come and lead him or her to the Western Paradise. This simple belief had already become influential in Lady Sarashina's time and, though Amidism was not yet a separate sect, the idea of salvation through faith, rather than through religious discipline, exercise, good works, etc., had already gained strong support (WSP, pp. 114–15).

213. The fingers could be bent and joined in various ways to symbolize the Buddha's Vow and other religious ideas. These arcane finger-signs, which derived from the ancient Indian mudras, were especially important in Esoteric Buddhism.

214. I.e., the sons of her dead sister, and also her late husband's nephews.

215. Rokuhara: residential district southeast of the Capital (map 3).

216. This is not one of the more brilliant poems in the book, but it is important in providing the only likely clue to the title. The poem is based on the following famous one in a tenth-century anthology:

> *Inconsolable my heart*
> *As I gaze upon the moon that shines*
> *On Sarashina's Mount Obasute.*

Obasute, which is the name of a famous mountain in Sarashina District in the Province of Shinano, has the literal meaning of "forsaken aunt" and in this poem to her nephew the author uses it to refer to her own sombre, desolate condition since her husband's death. There is not the slightest evidence that she herself ever visited Sarashina during her husband's brief term as Governor of Shinano, and the book contains no other reference to either Obasute or Sarashina. According to legend, Obasute was the mountain (or one of the mountains) where old people were abandoned to die when they had become an economic burden in their village community.

217. Overgrown sagebrush (*yomogi*) was a standard symbol for lonely desolation and was particularly associated with the silent, decaying houses of women who were no longer visited by men (cf. "The Palace in the Tangled Woods" in Arthur Waley's translation of *The Tale of Genji*. This chapter describes the desolate, broken-down house of Suetsumuhana, the gauche, red-nosed princess on whom Genji takes pity).